SCHOLASTIC

GUIDE TO

BALANCED READING

3–6

MAKING IT WORK FOR YOU

*Edited by Joyce Baltas, Ph.D.
and Susan Shafer, Ed.D.*

SCHOLASTIC
PROFESSIONAL BOOKS

NEW YORK • TORONTO • LONDON • AUCKLAND • SYDNEY

Cover design by Vincent Ceci and Jaime Lucero
Cover photograph by Grant Huntington for Scholastic Inc.
Interior design by Solutions by Design, Inc.

Copyright © 1996 by Scholastic Inc.
All rights reserved. Published by Scholastic Inc.

ISBN 0-590-96053-9
2 3 4 5 6 7 8 9 10   10   03 02 01 00 99 98 97 96
Printed in the U.S.A.

Contents

Introduction

Teaching reading has always engendered extensive discussion in the educational community. It has also stimulated a variety of instructional approaches. In the past decade, for example, there was a move towards literature-based instruction. Teachers put away their skills books and phonics lessons and filled their classrooms with large numbers of trade books. While the shift to the use of literature brought about an appreciation for real books, it did so at the expense of skills instruction.

What teachers realized was that areas such as phonemic awareness, phonics, and reading skills and strategies were critical to producing fluent, independent readers. There needed to be a balance between literature and intentional skills instruction.

The purpose of this book is to provide teachers and administrators with a theoretical base for creating a balanced reading program. *Balanced Reading* also gives educators a chance to step into actual classrooms where teachers have successfully implemented effective programs.

For each of the chapters in this book you will find four components:

- Spotlight on Theory
- Spotlight on Practice
- Assessing Your Classroom
- Try This

Spotlight on Theory provides the theoretical base and recommended instructional techniques for each topic. Spotlight on Practice offers concrete examples of the application of that area in the classroom.

Assessing Your Classroom is a tool for reflecting on classroom practice, while Try This suggests ways for teachers to reflect, evaluate and experiment with new approaches.

Balanced Reading can be used several ways:

- as a staff development tool
- as part of a teacher or administrator's professional library
- as a general resource for finding practical teaching ideas
- as a chance to "visit" with other classrooms and see how other teachers create balanced reading programs.

We hope this book is helpful to you and your students.

Joyce Baltas and Susan Shafer
Editors

A Balanced Reading Approach

Spotlight on THEORY

D. Ray Reutzel

Consider the goals of your classroom reading and writing program. Do you, like all teachers, hope your students will become independent, competent, thoughtful, and avid readers and writers? If so, you probably have already discovered that there is no single or simple route to achieving your goals. An effective literacy program requires a variety of approaches—carefully selected and balanced to ensure that children are regularly exposed to literature, a variety of reading materials, rich language experiences, and systematic instruction.

How do teachers design a balanced literacy program? They use what they know about independent, competent, thoughtful readers and writers to create an effective reading program. Such a program includes:

- Reading aloud on a daily basis **to** students, to foster a love of literature.

- Reading and writing **with** students using systematic, intentional skills and strategy instruction, based on the literature.

- Reading and writing **by** students, to help them achieve independence.

- Access to a variety of reading materials, such as fiction and nonfiction, maps, charts, graphs, references, technology, etc.

Classroom Libraries

For a program to be successful, children must have access to plenty of reading materials. Your classroom library, therefore, should be stocked with a minimum of 300 to 1,500 books, enough titles to entice students to always be absorbed in a good read. Studies have shown that time spent reading is a major factor in the improvement of upper-grade students' reading achievement (Anderson, R.C., Wilson, P. T., & Fielding L. G., 1988; Reutzel, D. R., & Hollingsworth, P., 1991).

Once you decide on the elements of your balanced literacy program, the next step is to consider the best ways to organize them within a framework that provides independent, small-group, and whole-class learning experiences.

Acquiring a Love of Literature: Reading To Students

Teacher Read Alouds

It is remarkable how something as easy and pleasurable as hearing stories and poems read aloud on a daily basis can be so worthwhile to students. Peterson and Eeds (1990) see teachers who share good literature with their students as "helping [children] see [works of art] in ways they may not have discovered on their own" (p.12), noticing language, structure, sequence, and style. Encouraging children to think of similar possibilities for their own writing is the next logical step. Soon children begin to read other texts more critically and through the eyes of an author. In this way, children become writers because they are readers. They become better readers because they are writers.

Achieving Competence: Reading and Writing with Others

Core Literature

In a core literature approach, an anthology of selections such as those found in basal readers is the focus of instruction for the group. Unlike the basal readers of past years, however, anthologies today offer original works of literature and a variety of genres, writing styles, and themes. At all grade levels, core literature offers many opportunities for incorporating reading and writing and for the integration of language arts.

Systematic, planned skills instruction is a key element of the balanced reading approach. By using this approach that is connected to the text, students are taught a wide variety of skills needed to become fluent, strategic readers. Skill instruction also focuses on the author's use of language, on writing techniques, and on literary devices. After locating and reading examples of the techniques authors use, students should begin to think of ways to apply them to their own writing.

Literature Circles

Discussion groups—such as literature circles, book clubs, and novel groups— allow students, in groups of two to six, to meet regularly. In those groups, youngsters explore their ideas about a trade book or anthology selection through "genuine conversation among real readers" (Wyshynski and Paulsen, 1995, p.263).

One way teachers form groups is by presenting "talks" on several trade books and inviting students to choose one book to read. This strategy may produce heterogeneous groups, and collaborations between proficient and less-proficient readers often help students function well (Moore, 1995).

Several excellent discussion formats are possible. In a Collaborative Reasoning approach (Waggoner, Chinn, Yi, and Anderson, 1995), for example, central discussion questions are constructed by the teacher "to elicit alternative perspectives for which evidence can be found in the text" (p. 583). In an alternative approach, teachers ask group members to prepare their own questions and topics for each discussion by thinking about puzzling and surprising situations in the story as well as personal or literary experiences the novel brings to mind.

Achieving Independence: Reading and Writing By Students

Reading and Writing

No matter what you call your independent reading time, such as SSR (Silent Sustained Reading) or DEAR (Drop Everything and Read), it is grounded in the belief that anyone—children or adults—gets better at anything they practice regularly.

There are many factors for teachers to consider when organizing students' independent and reading time, but common to all are the elements of time, choice, and response (Atwell, 1987; Calkins, 1986; Graves, 1993). Students need regular chunks of time to read and write texts of their own choice independently, and to respond to those works.

Response Journals or Notebooks

One of the best ways to help children make sense of a story is to ask them to write their interpretations and reactions in a notebook or journal (Atwell, 1987; Wollman-Bonilla, 1994). After they make inferences about what they have read, suggest that they prove their points by referring to the text or their own knowledge and experiences. ("What makes you think that will happen?") Because the exploration of ideas presents more risks and challenges than merely writing plot summaries, you will need to establish a climate that encourages risk taking and trust. When you introduce response journals, therefore, invite your students to write their opinions, thoughts, and questions about books without worrying about mechanics.

Mini-lessons

Mini-lessons provide excellent opportunities for whole-class instruction on literary elements, writers' techniques, vocabulary, the mechanics and conventions of written language, and skills and strategies for comprehending reading and composing writing. Models and demonstrations often make the most effective teaching tools. For example, if your purpose is to introduce reading journals or to improve the quality of your students' responses, you could read aloud several examples of thoughtful journal entries (including your own). Help children see that thoughtful entries offer reasons or evidence from the text to support opinions.

Conferences

While demonstration helps students see how good readers and writers think, conferences are needed to help them apply what they've learned.

Writing conferences usually begin with the student's discussion of the text and with problems the writer may have experienced. The teacher's role is to react with questions and comments that will stretch the student's thinking, and to suggest options and strategies for solving the problems (Fiderer, 1993).

The reading conference is an ideal time to monitor independent reading, diagnose problems, and check for comprehension, fluency, and appropriateness of books. Students experiencing reading difficulties should be carefully instructed to apply the three skill systems of strategic reading: comprehension, phonics, and grammar cues.

CD-ROM Technology

Applications of CD-ROM technology offer new variations on the independent reading experience. Certain programs allow upper-elementary students the opportunity to read chapter books on CD-ROM in an engaging format. For example, a student reading a book about immigration can call up a video of actual people in history describing the possessions they brought with them on their trip to America.

Summary

A balanced reading program assures that all children receive a well-rounded exposure to good literature, rich language experiences, and systematic skill instruction in reading and writing. Such a program assists children in becoming strategic, socially interactive, competent, and independent readers and writers.

D. Ray Reutzel is the Karl G. Maeser Research Professor and Department Chair of Elementary Education, Brigham Young University; Board of Directors, College Reading Association.

References

Anderson, R. C., Wilson, P. T., & Fielding L. G. (1988). Growth in Reading and How Children Spend Their Time Outside of School. *Reading Research Quarterly*, 23(3), pp. 285–303.

Atwell, N. (1987). *In the Middle: Reading, Writing, and Learning with Adolescents*. Portsmouth, New Hampshire: Heinemann.

Calkins, L. (1986). *The Art of Teaching Writing*. Portsmouth, New Hampshire: Heinemann.

Fiderer, A. (1993). *Teaching Writing: A Workshop Approach*. New York: Scholastic.

Graves, D. (1993). *Writing: Teachers & Children at Work*. Portsmouth, New Hampshire: Heinemann.

Peterson, R. & Eeds, M. (1990). *Grand Conversations: Literature Groups in Action*. New York: Scholastic.

Reutzel, D. R. & Hollingsworth, P. (1991). Reading Time in School: Effect on Fourth-Graders' Performance on a Criterion-Referenced Comprehension Test. *Journal of Educational Research*, 84, (3), pp. 170–176.

Reutzel, D. R. and Cooter, R. B. (1991). "Organizing for Effective Instruction: The Reading Workshop." *Reading Teacher*, 44 (8), 548–555.

Rosenblatt, L. (1978). *The Reader, the Text, the Poem*. Carbondale: Southern Illinois University Press.

Routman, R. (1991). *Invitations*. Portsmouth, New Hampshire: Heinemann.

Wollman-Bonilla, J. (1994). *Response Journals: Inviting Students to Think and Write About Literature*. New York: Scholastic.

Waggoner, M., Chinn, C., Yi, H., and R. C. Anderson. (1995). "Collaborative Reasoning About Stories." *Language Arts*, Vol. 72, No. 8. pp. 582–589.

Wyshynski, R. and D. Paulsen. (1995) "Maybe I Will Do Something: Lessons from *Coyote*." *Language Arts*, Vol. 72, No. 4. pp. 258–264.

Spotlight on PRACTICE

Stella Perry

O ver twenty years ago when I first started teaching, I used a basal anthology as the heart of my reading instruction. Although I considered myself a good teacher, I sometimes questioned my teaching of skills and strategies in isolation, apart from the reading material itself. I also worried that I was giving my students few opportunities to write.

In the past several years, I've tried a more balanced approach to reading and writing instruction. Today, as a fifth-grade teacher, I incorporate trade books into my reading lessons. My students spend time each day reading on their own, reading with me, and being read to. I teach skills and strategies that flow from the literature. And writing has become a critical component in my language arts classroom. It is clear that my students love to read and write and do so proficiently and voraciously.

The middle school I teach in uses a departmental program, so I see my students for an 80-minute period, not the whole day. This long period is sufficient to allow me to incorporate a variety of reading approaches every day. A literature-based basal forms the core of my reading instruction, which I supplement with trade books and other reading materials.

Variety of Reading Materials

O ne of the most valuable resources I have is my classroom library. I have been adding to my library over the years, mostly by using grant money to order books through book clubs and by buying some trade books at yard sales. I also try to include a variety of other reading materials—magazines, newspapers, and real-life reading items such as bus schedules, maps, nonfiction books, nature guidebooks, and encyclopedias. Often, when we begin a new unit, I send letters to parents asking for resources that relate to our theme. Families have been quite responsive.

Reading and Writing to Students

I believe in reading to my students every day. Sometimes I read a novel, sometimes short stories, other times poetry. I try to chose material that relates to the theme we are studying. I often tape-record my reading so that students can listen to the story as they read on their own. This has worked well for my reluctant readers.

Some days I read to students for as long as thirty minutes. Often I read aloud a chapter, then ask students to read the next chapter silently. This is one way I can be sure that everyone reads independently every day.

I write to my students in several ways. Every day I write messages on the board. I also write to students in their dialogue journals. In addition, I leave messages for my students on the classroom computer.

A Diverse Assessment

Planning has been key to creating a balanced reading program in my room. I begin each year with several assessments to determine my students' reading and writing skills. For example, I use an interview to find out my students' interests and a family questionnaire to learn what children read and write at home.

I also ask students to submit a writing sample and a tape recording in which they read a selection orally. I also administer a placement test to determine the skills and strategies they most need.

I then review the stories in the basal, trade books, and expository texts my students will be reading to determine which skills and strategies can be taught from those materials. Based on the results of the placement tests, I group my students for skill instruction. As the need arises, I also teach a variety of mini-lessons on reading and writing skills.

Reading and Writing with Students

I have many good examples of the ways in which skills and strategies flow naturally from my students' literature anthology and trade books. *Julie of the Wolves* is a wonderful book from which to teach similes and metaphors.

In one section of the story Julie uses colors to describe memories. She remembers the old men sitting around the fire at the seal camp as golden brown. In class we had a great discussion about memories and color. As a follow-up, I asked the students to make a color wheel and divide it into sections. In each section students used a different color for a different memory. Then they wrote about the memory using the story as a model. I am always delighted by their descriptions. One boy wrote that the colors black and white remind him of his grandmother: every Sunday morning he and his grandmother deliver the newspaper!

When students in literature circles finish reading a book, I always involve them in a project. Recently, we were studying World War II. The students had read a variety of nonfiction and fiction works that relate to the war—*The Diary of Anne Frank, The Summer of My German Soldier,* and *Number the Stars*. At the end of the unit, two students wrote letters to each other in which they assumed the role of the main character in the stories. The letters were an alternative way to assess the girls' comprehension. By reading the letters I found out how much they understood about the times and the characters' personalities. Their comprehension was good.

Using Other Media

I like to use other media for reading and writing instruction. When we read the book *Hatchet,* we also watched the movie. Then the students formed small groups and compared and contrasted the two versions, which were significantly different from each other. This activity gave me additional insight into how much the students comprehended the book and the movie. When we discussed which they preferred I found that the students who love to read preferred the book "because of the rich details."

Reading and Writing by Students

I have built into our schedule a time each day for students to read silently. Usually they read the book from their literature circle. Students also write daily in their response journals.

Our district has been engaged in writing process for quite a few years. By the time students arrive in my class they are comfortable with the writing process and are eager to write. We use the stories they read as models for their writing.

After they read and watched *Hatchet* we used both media as a model for writing an adventure story. One of my recent lessons focused on the elements of an adventure story. We went back into the story to find examples of each element (plot, action, characterization, and others). The students then applied what they learned about adventure stories to their own writing. My lessons on grammar, usage, mechanics, and spelling instruction came from the students' work.

Cross Age Teaching

For several years I have had my students participate in a program in which we read to the kindergarten students at a nearby school. I have found that not only do my students enjoy the activity, but their reading abilities have greatly improved as a result.

This has been particularly helpful for my more reluctant readers. Because they are reading to kindergartners, they choose simple stories with a great deal of picture support. At the beginning of the project I modeled how to read aloud. I demonstrated what makes an effective read aloud (good expression, glancing up at the audience, variation in voice).

My students spend a lot of time rehearsing. This gives my reluctant readers a chance to practice reading easy texts in a nonthreatening environment. Because we are in a middle school, we did not have access to picture books so I brought in books from home, from yard sales, and from the public library. Last year we received a $300 grant to buy books for our read-aloud program. I found that this program has improved my student's attitude about reading, and their confidence as readers has increased. This year my class decided that they should also write some original stories to read to the kindergartners. These books are now part of the kindergarten library.

Summary

I have found that by using a literature-based balanced reading program my fifth-graders have become more fluent readers. Because literature is a basis for skill and strategy instruction, my students have had an easier time learning and applying new skills. In addition, our kindergarten partnership has given my students a new sense of purpose for reading and increased their self-esteem. A balanced reading program has improved my students' love of reading, learning, and teaching.

Stella Perry teaches in the Bridgeton Middle School in Bridgeton, New Jersey.

References

Frank, A. (1994). *The Diary of a Young Girl.* New York: Knopf.

George, J. C. (1972). *Julie of the Wolves.* New York: HarperCollins.

Greene, B. (1973). *The Summer of My German Soldier.* New York: Dial Books for Young Readers.

Lowry, L. (1989). *Number the Stars.*, Boston, MA: Houghton Mifflin.

Paulsen, G. (1986). *Hatchet.* Old Tappan, NJ: Macmillan.

Assessing Your Classroom

	Yes	Some	No
1 Do you use a wide range of literature and a variety of reading materials (maps, encyclopedias, brochures)?			
2 Do you have between 300 and 1,500 books in your classroom library?			
3 Do you give your students daily independent reading time?			
4 Do you use mini-lessons to teach literary elements, writer's techniques, vocabulary, and skills and strategies for reading comprehension?			
5 Do you use teacher-student conferences for both reading and writing?			
6 Do you have technology that supports students as both readers and writers?			
7 Do you plan and execute systematic skills instruction?			
8 Do you read aloud to your students on a daily basis?			
9 Do students meet and discuss books read in literature circles and book clubs?			
10 Do the skills and strategies that you teach stem from the students' reading and writing?			
11 Do you have a balanced reading program?			

Try This

① Assess Your Classroom

Evaluate your current reading program. Is it balanced? Make a list of ways it *is* balanced (see Assessing Your Classroom, page 16) and the ways in which it can be enriched. Choose one area that you would like to work on (for example, establishing literature circles) and incorporate it into your Integrated Language Arts program. After one month, reevaluate and determine if there is an area you'd like to add or modify.

② Hold a Book Drive

Survey the books in your classroom library to see if there is a balanced selection. Is there fiction and nonfiction, magazines, newspapers, realia (for example, maps, bus schedules, guidebooks) and reference materials? Enlist the help of families in acquiring the kinds of materials you and the class would like. Make a master list and distribute it to families. You may also place the list on a school bulletin board and request donations.

③ Plan Skills Instruction

Are the skills and strategies you teach in your lessons truly coming from the literature you teach? Make a list of the stories and trade books you'll be teaching in the next few months and the skills and strategies that naturally support the text. Prioritize the skills and strategies and target two or three. Identify those that lend themselves well to mini-lessons, and teach them in short lessons during the next few weeks.

2

Managing Your Classroom

Spotlight on **THEORY**

Delores Stubblefield Seamster

Successful classroom managers use a variety of materials and activities to teach students who often function within a broad range of ability levels. This article presents research and practical suggestions for helping you, the teacher, manage a classroom in which learning is maximized for all students.

A Demanding Situation

Implementing a balanced reading program is often a complex task. Teachers need to do many things at once. They must

- establish and manage multiple objectives (district and state objectives, for example);
- plan systematic instruction based on assessment;
- use flexible grouping to meet instructional needs;
- plan and establish routines that allow for ongoing assessment;
- establish procedures for accessing materials.

Establish Goals and Objectives

An extensive body of research suggests that effective reading programs in classrooms are characterized by specific instruction of clearly defined objectives (Anderson, Evertson, & Brophy, 1979; Delpit, 1988). Therefore, the first stage of classroom planning should involve a careful analysis of school, local, and state literacy goals. Teachers often feel frustrated when faced with the prospect of teaching every student every possible concept embedded in a book or short story selection. With so many time constraints, some teachers just "mention" literacy concepts without providing the kind of systematic instruction students need to master new reading strategies.

Good classroom managers avoid this dilemma by carefully planning systematic instruction based on an identified scope of goals and objectives and on students' needs. This means that effective managers do not leave essential instruction to chance. Their lessons reflect much forethought.

Assess Reading and Writing Objectives

After setting goals and objectives, effective classroom managers begin the school year with an assessment of students' reading abilities. For example, grades 4–6 teachers at N.W. Harrlee always enhance the results of standardized reading tests by giving a class placement test and then doing further diagnosis with informal reading inventories early in the fall term. They also collect students' writing samples to get a picture of their writing abilities.

Recently, the teachers were surprised to find that the standardized test scores didn't always provide a complete record of students' strengths and weaknesses. In fact, teachers often discovered a number of additional strengths and deficiencies for some students. With this added information, teachers used the results of their informal reading inventories to plan for differentiated activities based on individual student needs. As the year went on, the teachers maintained an accurate picture of each student's individual reading ability by conducting ongoing assessment.

A Fine Example
Fourth-grade teacher Karla Johnson knows how to plan for a balanced reading classroom. First she decides on a lesson focus designed to draw the whole class into their planned encounter with literacy. The focus includes:

- setting purposes for reading;

- building background knowledge;

- relating the learning to student interests and experiences.

Next, she uses the plan to outline the strategies, techniques, and materials that she will need to deliver instruction, giving careful consideration to extension and enrichment activities required to meet individual student needs. Finally, the plan she creates addresses strategies for ongoing assessment of the learner.

This kind of planning usually results in suggestions for a number of materials and activities appropriate for accomplishing the lesson objectives. The plan takes into account students' different interests, abilities, and motivations.

Use Flexible Grouping

The use of flexible groups becomes a valuable management technique in a balanced reading program. It can help a teacher maximize each student's progress.

There are various ways to group students and each serves a different worthwhile purpose. During the course of a day, there are times when the whole class comes together, when students work as individuals, when partners or small groups complete tasks, and when larger, cooperative groups assemble. The formation of groups is based on many different criteria:

- skill groups: students who work together on mastering a specific skill or strategy;

- interest groups: students who share a particular interest;

- homogeneous groups: students who are at the same level;

- heterogeneous groups: students who are at various levels.

Some teachers find that for practice, homogeneous skill groupings work best. Examples of such groupings are: Extra Support, Teacher Support, Collaborative, and Independent.

Although most writing is done independently, students meet in small groups to share and revise their work. These groupings can be heterogeneous, with more proficient students helping those less proficient.

For many of the teachers I work with, interest groups prove successful for integrated curriculum activities and for workshops and projects.

Just as teachers rearrange their spatial organization according to the changing needs of their students, they can also use flexible grouping to accommodate fluctuating needs and to enrich their students' classroom experience.

Helpful Guidelines

Although many researchers support some use of grouping in the classroom (Helman, Blair, & Rupley, 1990; MacDonald, 1991), certain guidelines must be considered if groups are to provide differentiated instruction for all learners.

1. Groups should be flexible and formed according to common student interests and abilities, rather than just grouped by test scores.

2. Students must be encouraged to move freely between groups as appropriate for the learning task. This approach to grouping helps to avoid the creation of social divisions within a classroom that can harm both proficient and less-proficient readers.

Deborah Proctor, for example, handles grouping very well in her third-grade classroom. Each day she works with small *homogeneous* groups of students that have special needs for skills instruction. In addition, Deborah groups students *heterogeneously* for planned extension activities such as writing and integrating language arts activities.

Ongoing Assessment

Because children's needs continually fluctuate, ongoing assessment must be an integral part of classroom management. Deborah uses ongoing assessment to customize instruction for the students in her small homogeneous groups. The assessment process ensures that each student receives instruction that best meets his or her changing needs.

Establish Routines

Research indicates that effective teachers rely on classroom routines to make effective use of classroom time while creating a climate conducive to learning. Such routines are particularly useful for ensuring that students become engaged in authentic learning tasks when first entering the classroom each morning.

For example, most upper-elementary students can be taught to engage in sustained silent reading, journal writing, or buddy reading during the first few minutes of class each day.

Once instruction is in progress, effective routines can help teachers with the management of flexible reading groups. As the teacher works with one small group, the other students must be engaged in meaningful independent literacy tasks.

For example, good classroom managers might develop a class signal (playing chimes, for example) to be used in situations when the teacher needs complete student attention. Such a signal permits the teacher, if necessary, to quickly and efficiently communicate to students who are engaged in various activities throughout the classroom.

A powerful routine that maximizes time on task and reduces the loss of student learning time during transitions is the use of independent reading. Students are taught to read for pleasure when they are between assignments or when tasks are completed early. According to researchers, independent reading helps students increase their reading proficiency while developing a love for reading (Krashen, 1993).

The teachers at Wheatley Elementary have taken steps to ensure that this works in their school. Reading nooks are set up in the classrooms and students are invited to curl up with a book when their assignments are finished.

Students Help Out

Classroom routines should be extended to include the use of student helpers. In a balanced reading program there are a number of activities or chores that can be delegated to students. For example, students can put folded homework and other written assignments in a designated place on their desks throughout the day. A student helper can be assigned to collect the work at specific times each day. If the assignments are not in the designated place on the desk, the helper simply moves on, "no questions asked." The student helper can be taught to pick up the papers quickly and quietly, permitting the rest of the class to continue working on their learning activities.

Procedures For Accessing Materials

Establishing procedures can also help manage students' access to the wide variety of supplementary materials that make up a balanced reading program. In many classrooms, certain items must be centrally located for common use by the entire class. When encyclopedias, atlases, almanacs, periodicals, computers, tape recorders, and other learning materials must be shared during independent student use, explicit routines should be established for accessing these items. This minimizes classroom distractions and maximizes student time on-task.

Felicia Knight, a third-grade teacher at Johnston Elementary School, keeps encyclopedias, trade books, and dictionaries on a shelf in front of the classroom. She limits to four the number of students who get out of their seats for materials at one time. After choosing a book or other resource from a central location for leisure use, Ms. Knight's students are required to keep their selections for the given period of time before making an alternate choice (a minimum of ten minutes, for example).

The "minimum time" rule can be integrated with the four at a time guideline to create an effective classroom climate that fosters student independence and choice. It also promotes an efficient use of student learning time.

The goal of effective classroom management should always be kept in mind when planning and establishing classroom routines. Teachers should recognize that the overriding purpose for these activities is to create and maintain a positive climate for literacy.

Delores Stubblefield Seamster is Principal of N.W. Harrlee Elementary School in Dallas, Texas.

Reference

Krashen, S. D. (October 1993). The Case for Free Voluntary Reading. *Canadian Modern Language Reveiw*, 72–82.

Spotlight on **PRACTICE**

Donald Dale Valle

When I begin a new school year I involve my fifth-grade students as much as possible in the management of the classroom. After all, for the next nine months this will be my students' home away from home, and it is important that they have a stake in planning and implementing the procedures I except them to adopt. I think in advance about the basic framework of my classroom organizational plan—the rules, consequences of breaking them, seating arrangements, and daily routines. But from the very first day of school, I always give students the opportunity to offer their input about these important issues.

Getting Started

We usually start by brainstorming situations that students feel have hindered their learning in the past. The kids are wonderful at this task. They point out situations that teachers may not be aware of, such as noisy games at the computer or excessive, and therefore distracting, use of the pencil sharpener. We use this input to formulate our classroom rules. Interestingly, in the six years I've used this approach students themselves have never failed to mention the problems of classmates' talking too loudly or casual "walking by" their desks, diverting their attention from completing assignments. They say these are disruptions to learning.

Procedures

Following our discussion, I guide the class to formulate rules and routines that will help prevent distractions and maximize academic time-on-task. Again, I encourage students' input. They usually come up with more and stricter rules than I do. The key is that these rules are "our rules," not just "my rules." Consequently, students feel real ownership of their classroom environment and are much more likely to maintain a positive climate for learning. It is a democratic process that has beneficial results.

Modifications Based on Practice

I then turn to monitoring the physical arrangement of the classroom. Prior to the first day of school, I make student seating assignments, set up computer stations, and arrange resources (such as encyclopedias and trade books) so they are easily accessible. Once classes begin, I carefully observe the physical setting for two or three weeks. My observation gives me a chance to see what works—and what doesn't.

One year I set up computers in a position that looked fine before school started. After a week I realized that the heads of students working independently at the computer blocked the view of the assignments printed on the front board. I made suitable changes.

Another time I set up a place in the room for small group instruction. After two weeks I discovered that the arrangement was poor. My table—where instruction involved conversation and lots of back and forth between teacher and students—was too close to other students working independently at their desks. As I interacted with the small groups, other students ignored their independent tasks and listened instead to the small group discussion nearby. I rearranged classroom seating to maximize learning for both groups.

Be Adaptable

I have found that the key to good classroom management is flexibility. Rules, routines, and physical arrangements should be monitored and adjusted continuously in order to maintain an environment that supports literacy. There is an old saying: "Rules are made to be broken." That's not entirely true, but they certainly are made to be modified or changed when needed. My advice? Don't be afraid to change things if they aren't working. A well-managed classroom should not mean a rigid place that restricts student learning. Instead, it should be an inviting setting that makes learning fun for both the teacher and students.

Donald Dale Valle teaches in the N. W. Harrlee Elementary School in Dallas, Texas.

Assessing Your Classroom

	Yes	Some	No
1 Have you established your literacy goals for the year?			
2 Do you use a variety of assessment procedures, such as placement tests, benchmark books, observations, checklists, portfolios, standardized tests, and so forth?			
3 Have you established procedures for morning routines, such as putting away coats or checking homework?			
4 Have you established a system for children to borrow books from the classroom library?			
5 When students complete an assignment, is there a choice of other independent or small group constructive activities from which they can select?			
6 In the writing center, have you established a workable system for accessing paper, editing checklists, date stamp, and other materials?			
7 Have you established a system for storing works-in-progress?			
8 Do students have a predictable time and day for writing?			
9 Do you use flexible groups to meet a variety of student needs?			

Try This

Base Classroom Routines and Organization on Student Needs and Suggestions.

Follow these steps to create an orderly, organized classroom that maximizes learning in a balanced reading program.

(1) Make a map of your classroom.

> Use symbols to show the location of desks, shelves, globes, computers, library books, and other items designated for student use. Keep a record of paths used most often by students during the day. Also, note those resources and materials that are used most frequently.

(2) Next, conduct a meeting with your students.

> Distribute classroom maps to each child. Share your observations of high-traffic routes and most frequently used resources.

(3) Ask students to help you develop classroom routines that will minimize distractions and maximize academic learning.

> Talk about ways to improve the present plan. In short, formulate an effective classroom environment that incorporates students' suggestions with your own. Post these on a wall or bulletin board and ask students to follow them.

Repeat the process every few months to ensure that arrangements continue to meet the changing needs of your class.

3

Assessing Your Classroom

Spotlight on THEORY

by Adele Fiderer

Consider for a moment the different ways you assess your students as they write, read, and talk about books. Perhaps early in the year you prepared a survey to learn about students' interests and backgrounds as readers and writers. Then too, you may have asked students to save samples of their work, or made notes while listening to a child read aloud.

If you have taken any of these measures and interpreted the data, you probably have already discovered how useful these assessments are for managing a multifaceted literacy program. In this article I will discuss a range of assessment options from ongoing, informal assessment to formal assessment through testing.

Early Decisions

There are many questions that may come to mind regarding assessment. For example: How do you decide which student samples to assess? Which assessment strategies and tools work best? How can children and parents become part of the assessment process?

One good way to answer these is to think about the areas of learning you value and want to know more about. Then select a variety of measures—formal, ongoing, and informal—for obtaining information.

You also need to consider the best times for conducting assessments during the year. Your informal performance assessments will be ongoing as you gather data developed during your students' daily learning activities. Additional assessments, both informal (teacher-designed inventories and tasks) and formal (standardized tests) are usually conducted at particular points during the year. Figure 1 shows an example of a useful assessment planning chart.

What do I value and want to know more about?	Assessments (Strategies, tools)	Figure 1
Reading comprehension	one-to-one reading conference records, literacy journals, written comprehension tasks, scoring rubrics and benchmarks, placement tests, unit tests, mid-year and end-of-year tests	
Reading/writing background, interests	student and family surveys and interviews, book records, literacy journals, profile forms	
Learning new words	one-to-one reading conference records, miscue analyses, vocabulary tests	
Core Reading Groups	benchmark books for diagnosis, discussion questions, conferences, benchmarks	
Literature Circle discussions	students' questions, teachers' observational records, surveys, student evaluations of group	
Literary devices and elements	fiction writing samples, teacher-designed tests, rubrics	
Writing	one-to-one conference records, writing samples, portfolios, student-peer-parent evaluation forms, writing tasks, benchmarks	
Spelling, usage, grammar and mechanics	writing samples, proofreading tasks, usage, grammar, spelling tests	

Formal Assessment

Formal assessment can provide valuable information to help you plan and group for instruction. *Placement tests* administered in the beginning of the year allow you to diagnose children's vocabulary knowledge, and reading and writing abilities. *Unit tests* help you determine the skills and strategies students have mastered. Unit tests also focus on the skills and strategies you might reteach during the next unit. *End-of-year tests* provide information on students' growth in reading and writing. These tests form an important part of the overall assessment process.

Informal Assessment

For performance assessment to be meaningful, you will need a clear idea of your goals for your students. Once that has been decided, you can ask yourself, "How is each student doing? What can I do to help each child reach the learning target?"

Your next challenge is to find appropriate ways to judge your students' performances and demonstrations fully, consistently, and effectively. Here are three effective ways to meet these challenges.

Developmental Models

A developmental model displays sequential stages of development in a given curriculum area. Descriptors, or learning behaviors, illustrate each stage.

Reading and writing developmental models allow teachers to better articulate to themselves and to parents the developmental stages that occur within and across grades. They also give teachers and parents a common language for talking about literacy growth. Because a developmental model provides information about several stages, from earliest reading to proficient, you will be able to identify the stage that best describes what each child can do. Here, for example, is a description of a fluent reader.

A Fluent Reader:

- selects, reads, and completes a wide variety of materials with guidance
- uses reference materials independently
- identifies and discusses literary elements and genre motifs with guidance
- uses evidence to justify opinions with guidance
- recognizes and imitates styles of favorite authors

Information like this informs your assessment process in several ways. First, it points to specific behaviors and capabilities that you might want to focus on when observing a child's performance. Second, it provides a road map that shows where your students have been, where they are now, and what they should be reaching for next. Knowing what students need to learn will help you plan instruction—surely a major benefit of assessment.

Portfolios

Used in various ways from kindergarten through college, portfolios are collections of student work created through authentic learning activities over time. Although portfolios usually include samples showing student's best work, they also include "before" and "after" samples that reflect change and growth.

For portfolios to be meaningful to children, certain conditions should be met:

- The selection of entries should be an ongoing process, rather than a one-time event.

- Students should be at the center of the portfolio assessment process. Students should choose work samples for their portfolios and explain why those items belong there.

You can help your students become reflective assessors of their work by demonstrating the selection process you might go through if the portfolio were yours. For example, you might think-aloud your reasons for placing a response log entry in the folder (or shoebox or envelope), using criteria that you and your students develop together. Then encourage your students to keep the criteria in mind as they reread and reevaluate their log entries in search of their "best" work to date.

Rubrics

Holistic evaluation scales or rubrics based on specific criteria offer an excellent way to interpret and evaluate writing projects. They also provide a benchmark for student performance.

Rubrics have another advantage. Showing students a rubric makes your expectations clear before students begin to write. This helps youngsters produce better work.

Imagine how helpful the following rubric on story comprehension was for the teachers and students who used it. In this case, students were asked to respond to the prompt: *Write about an important problem in the story. Tell why it was important and how it was solved.*

Score	Response	Figure 2
3 (Outstanding)	The written response is complete. It indicates a very good understanding of the story and its problem. It provides accurate, relevant details, information, and supportive reasoning.	
2 (Proficient)	The response is partial and indicates a fairly good understanding of the story. The information selected includes mostly accurate details and ideas. Some may be inaccurate or unrelated to a story's problem.	
1 (Apprentice)	The response is fragmentary and indicates only minimal understandings. It may include random details and irrelevant information.	
0 (Novice)	There is little or no response, or inaccurate and irrelevant details indicate a serious misunderstanding of the story.	

This (Figure 3) shows the rubric designed for scoring student's predictions about a story.

Score	Response	Figure 3
3 (Outstanding)	The response is complete. The prediction is logical and indicates an excellent understanding of the character and story events.	
2 (Proficient)	The response is partial. The prediction is logical and indicates a fairly good understanding of the story. The response relates to only one part of the story.	
1 (Apprentice)	The response is fragmentary. The prediction is barely connected to the story and indicates minimal understanding of the story's events and characters.	
0 (Novice)	The response is illogical. The prediction indicates serious misunderstanding of the story.	

Sharing Information with Families

To open doors to further communication, offer families a variety of times and places to talk with you about children's literacy. You may want to set up family conferences on the telephone, on E-mail, in home visits, or in the classroom itself. Your school may need to use flexible scheduling to accommodate families' work times.

During the conferences, share a variety of items with families, including portfolios with examples of projects completed and audio tapes of student's reading and writing, and results of placement and unit tests, and standardized tests.

Final Thoughts

A well-planned and balanced assessment process pays important dividends to you and your students. Formal and informal tools offer multiple indicators and data for making sound evaluations about your students' literacy growth. Measures such as portfolios, collaborative projects, and individual work samples show students how to look carefully at their work over time. Students' self-evaluations, based on knowledge of the criteria that informs your evaluations, helps youngsters identify their own strengths, their progress, and their goals for the future .

Adele Fiderer is a is an educational consultant and writer, and has been a classroom teacher in Scarsdale, New York and Los Angeles, California.

Spotlight on PRACTICE

by Kathy Ott

Then and Now

I've been a teacher in grades 4 to 6 for ten years. During that time, my assessment practices evolved from almost exclusive use of formal tests, to a greater balance between formal and informal methods.

Informal assessment has many dimensions. It includes:

- my observation of children's progress;
- students' portfolios or notebooks;
- students' writing samples;
- self- and peer assessment.

Both formal and informal assessment help me in planning meaningful lessons and activities for my students.

The Year Begins

In the beginning of the year, I start formally by administering multiple-choice tests in reading and language arts. The placement tests give me an idea of each child's level and the lessons I need to teach in immediate and future weeks.

These forms of assessment help me plan instruction by showing me students' strengths and weaknesses. If, for example, a pretest indicates that most students have already mastered the material in a unit, I know that I can spend a shorter time on that unit, lending extra support to the few students who need it. If most of the students do poorly on a test or quiz, I know that I should reteach that subject or skill.

Portfolio Assessment and Observation

Within a few weeks portfolio assessment and observation play a notable role in my classroom. The students often work on their portfolios, pulling things out, talking about why they've included or omitted a particular item, and explaining, in written or verbal form, what they were trying to do in writing a particular piece.

I also observe students regularly in a variety of groupings—noting strengths and areas in which they may require more support.

Involving Families

Communication between home and school is enhanced by assessment because assessment results show the degree of progress, as well as the areas that need strengthening, within each individual student. When interpreted, assessment results enable me to send home detailed letters about how each child is doing. When parents are better informed about their children's work and progress, they can work in further concert with me and support their children at home.

Self- and Peer Assessment

These assessment tools are helpful and enlightening. With peer-conferencing students work in writing workshop groups to bounce ideas off one another. In reading workshops, each student writes a letter after finishing a book. Then students meet with partners to share their letters before turning in their work.

In a weekly self-assessment session, I ask students to write one significant learning experience they had during the previous week. Once a month, I ask them to write what they learned in a particular content area ("Now I can use quotation marks correctly in writing") and where they think they need more work ("I'm still lost when it comes to spelling words with *ei* and *ie*"). I am always very impressed with how accurate and honest students are with these assessments. They really assume a lot of responsibility for their own learning.

Both peer assessment and self-assessment have advantages. With peer assessment, students learn to rely on each other. At times, they even raise issues or points that I had missed.

With peer assessment, students learn to cooperate and help one another. With self-assessment, students learn to rely on themselves, to view themselves honestly. Both forms of assessment are of great personal significance for the students and for me.

Kathy Ott teaches at the Delaware Academy in Syracuse, New York.

Assessing Your Classroom

Take time to reflect on your current approaches and consider which you are satisfied with and which you can strenghten.

	Yes	Some	No
1 Balanced Assessment			
Does my assessment system balance formal and informal techniques?			
Does my assessment system adequately represent student's development of reading (especially comprehension) and writing?			
2 Formal Assessment			
Do I use placement tests and unit test results to plan instruction and determine grouping?			
Do I share results of tests with families?			
3 Developmental Models, Portfolios and Rubrics			
Do I have a developmental model that describes the stages of students' reading and writing growth?			
Do I use rubrics to help score performance assessments?			
Have I established portfolios for each student?			
Have I set up a place to store documentation of group projects?			
Do I use a variety of forms of documentation— audio tapes, photographs, computer work, student's work, and my own notes?			
Am I satisfied with the criteria used to select student's work for their portfolios?			
Does my documentation of group projects reflect the variety of activities and projects in which students engage?			
Does my documentation of individual children's work adequately reflect their experiences and development?			
4 Involving Children and Families			
Do I involve students in the assessment process by meeting with them individually? Do I review with them their suggestions for their portfolios and for overall progress?			
Do I display photographs and documentation of group projects for students and visitors to see?			
Do I meet regularly with family members to share observations and assessments of their children's progress?			

Try This

① **Collect "exhibits" of special projects or events in which students participate. Use them as a way to record literacy events from beginning to end.** These can be a powerful tool when treated with value and shared with children and families.

- Start documenting a project from its inception. Take photographs of children planning the project, and ask children to keep lists of their initial ideas and suggestions. Provide a tape recorder for children to record their conversations.

- Next, photograph children working. Guide them to write lists and take notes about what they are doing.

- Collect children's works keeping early "drafts", as well as the final creation.

- When the project is completed, organize the documentation chronologically and display along with materials such as photographs, charts, notes, etc.

② **Establish a lending library. Invite families to borrow books and listen to children's reading.**

- Collect a variety of appropriate books. Create a library system, with a check-in/check-out form for children and family members to use.

- Create a chart with pockets each large enough to insert a standard index card. On the chart write the name of each child and family.

- On one index card each, write the title and author's name of each book. Attach card pockets to each book.

- When children or family members take out a book they can place the book's card in their pocket on the chart. When they return the book, they put the card back in the book.

    You can also create and distribute a catalog, listing the titles of all of the books available for families to borrow. Identify the type of book (picture book, story, folk tale, informational books) and a short description of the book's contents.

- Have a meeting with family members to introduce the new library system. Offer family members tips on listening to their children's read alouds. Suggestions may include:

- Do children's word substitutions make sense in the context of the story?

- Do children's word substitutions sound like the words in the text?

- Do children try to correct their own errors?

- With what kinds of words do children have the most trouble?

- Do children pay attention to punctuation?

    Encourage family members to note the above observations and to bring their notes to the next conference to discuss with you.

4

Integrating the Language Arts

Spotlight on THEORY

Gwendolyn Y. Turner

What is Integrated Language Arts?

Integrated Language Arts is a way of organizing learning that involves children in the study and use of the language arts components—reading, writing, speaking, listening, and viewing—as a unified core of concepts and activities. In an Integrated Language Arts classroom instruction is organized around a theme. All the reading, writing, listening, speaking and viewing then comes from and centers on the theme. A visitor to an integrated language arts classroom will probably witness the following scenario:

- Children are reading a wide variety of narrative and expository materials.

- Children are writing or revising stories, reports, poetry, or journal entries.

- Children are discussing, listening, and sharing information,

- Many children are completing projects in small groups, with partners, or independently.

- Children are learning from one another as well as from their teacher as they research topics, dramatize stories, create artwork, play vocabulary games, and rewrite story endings.

- The teacher is modeling learning, providing feedback, and helping children overcome learning barriers.

There is always a buzz of activities taking place in these classrooms. They are wonderful places for learning because they provide supportive environments in which children's creative voices are heard and in which both children and teachers celebrate learning. These classrooms integrate the language arts.

A Teacher in Action

I recall Kathy Hammer's third-grade classroom in St. Louis, Missouri, as a place for exciting learning. She helps her students construct meaning and communicate more effectively by integrating the language arts across the curriculum. While reading dePaola's wonderful story, *Strega Nona*, for example, her students dramatize and illustrate scenes, create magic potion recipes, use reference books to map out and plan a journey to Italy, keep a travel log of their trip, and write news accounts of their excursion.

Walmsley and Walp (1990) contend that reading and writing abilities are deeply rooted in the development of oral language knowledge, listening, and speaking and this is reflected in Hammer's classroom, as she uses reading, writing, speaking, and listening within and across the curriculum. In her classroom, for example, children read and write about wonderful stories such as *Happy Birthday Moon*, *Hundred Penny Box*, *Chrysanthemum*, and *Knots on a Counting Rope*. Through these books the children explore their own personal histories, dreams, and family traditions.

How Does Integrating the Language Arts Support a Balanced Reading Program?

An ideal classroom offers a well-designed instructional program and has a rich literacy environment. In such a classroom, children explore a variety of narrative and expository text material as they are exposed to a balanced reading program. This balanced reading program provides quality reading materials, excellent teacher modeling and mentoring, and meaningful learning experiences, along with daily opportunities to read, think, write, and discuss. When students make reading and writing connections across the curriculum, learning is more meaningful and less fragmented.

In sixth-grade teacher Ted Green's classroom we see evidence of a meaningful connectedness. As youngsters read books such as Seymour Simon's *New Questions and Answers About Dinosaurs*, these inquisitive students explore the reasons why dinosaurs became extinct. In addition, students in the classroom use a computer network to research topics, interact with scientists, complete research reports, and share their findings. Through their questioning, reading, researching, discussions, and writings, these students are exploring their universe. Green's students benefit from a variety of reading and writing tools as well as technology. The sixth-graders build their own communication skills through integrating learning and hands-on applications.

Basics of an Integrated Language Arts Program

In an Integrated Language Arts classroom, opportunities for both reading and writing abound. Reading and writing are complementary processes: Reading helps children assimilate the language structures they need in order to write; writing helps children develop concepts about written language that they need in order to read. Instruction in grammar, usage, and mechanics and spelling are taught intentionally and systematically, and comes from the writing that children are doing.

What Classroom Practice Supports an Integrated Language Arts Program?

Centers Make a Difference

An ideal classroom also uses listening, reading, research, and writing activities and centers to provide students with daily opportunities to use their language processes.

(1) *The listening center* provides books on tape, homework reviews and explanations, oral histories, songs, interviews, and quotations. (2) *The reading and research activities centers* provide a variety of children's magazines, books, newspapers, reference materials, as well as the children's own personal stories and commentaries. (3) *The writing activities centers* offer an outlet for children to create and share notes, letters, poetry, short stories, math story problems, jokes, songs, and book reviews.

Writing All Around

Students' writing should be evident in an Integrated Language Arts classroom. In fact, I am often impressed by the work of Mrs. Makeda Vales who has promoted writing by ensuring that her students share their writing with others. She teaches writing, grammar, usage, and spelling in the context of reading to help her students understand that reading and writing are tools for learning. In Vales's fifth-grade class, students display their writings in the hallways of the school as well as in the classroom and in the school journal. Integrating the language arts allows her children to learn from one another.

In an Integrated Language Arts program children read an array of rich literature. This literature then serves as the instructional basis for the writing. Children study each selection to learn the elements it embodies. Children then write their own example of the selection genre or of an element, strategy, or theme from the selection. For example, fourth-grade students read an excerpt from Jean Craighead George's *The Moon of the Alligators*. The section they are reading gives descriptions of a swamp from the alligator's point of view. They study and discuss the ways in which the author wrote from the alligator's point of view. They are then given the opportunity to write their own story told from an animal's point of view.

Solve Vital Problems

Children also use their language processes as tools to make decisions, solve problems, explore new concepts, and make connections to their own lives. When children share information and work in teams, they learn to use each member's strengths to get the job done. Designing and creating a classroom newspaper is one way in which everyone participates in the decision-making process.

In addition, children learn to use their intuition, reasoning abilities, and problem-solving skills when they read mysteries, create new inventions, or rewrite the endings to stories. They explore new concepts as they gather information from a variety of resources, create informational packets, and analyze the usefulness of different points of view. Children also make connections to their own lives when they solve their own problems ("Can we find a way to fight less?"), help their families ("Let's make a grocery budget, Mom."), and inspire others to take action on problems in the school and community ("Please help us appoint a team to fight litter in the playground.").

Why Implement an Integrated Language Arts Program?

Reaching One Student, Helping Teachers Plan

Integrating language arts activities helps children to make connections in their learning and assists teachers in planning. Gamberg (1988) maintains that integrated language arts provides opportunities for children to learn and explore and can serve a range of pedagogic interests, from meeting the needs of a single student to conceiving and developing overall curricular plans.

Students Who Need Extra Help

Integrating the language arts may also help those students who have experienced challenges in their learning. Roser and colleagues (1990) indicate that such students benefit because they can develop their vocabulary and apply meaningful comprehension strategies. When students improve their comprehension, they improve their learning.

In these environments, students are not focusing on isolated events but are acknowledging the integration of learning and hands-on applications. One fourth-grader I know summed this up well. After researching and doing science experiments on hurricanes and reading *The Magic School Bus—Inside a Hurricane,* he loudly exclaimed, "This stuff is all connected."

Providing Purpose

An Integrated Language Arts program helps children to recognize that literacy serves a purpose in their lives and helps them to use their literacy tools to improve their own communication abilities. Children learn best when they participate in meaningful activities that connect their learning across disciplines.

Teach Through Themes

- Design the instructional programs so that students are exposed to themes. Teaching through themes shows students the interconnectedness of reading, writing, grammar, and spelling. Expose them to books, poetry, stories, films, photography, and music.

Base Projects on Our Lives

- Involve students in activities that connect learning to the important things in their lives: writing, reading, student newspapers, reading partnerships, journal writing, and special projects. With these, students communicate about meaningful experiences and thoughts in their lives.

Encourage Literacy Everywhere, All the Time

- Support uninterrupted silent reading time, storytelling, poetry reading, research fairs, and authors' corners.

Family and Community

- Work with families, libraries, organizations, and volunteers to promote literacy in the home, neighborhood, and school.

Gwendolyn Y. Turner is Associate Professor of Literacy Education, University of Missouri—St. Louis; Editorial Board, Reading Research and Instruction.

References

Cole, J. (1995). *The Magic School Bus—In the Eye of the Hurricane.* New York: Scholastic.

Gamberg, R., Kwak, W., Hutchings, M. & Altheim, J. (1988). *Learning and Loving It: Theme Studies in the Classroom:* Portsmouth, New Hampshire: Heinemann.

George, J. C. (1991). *The Moon of the Alligators.* New York: HarperCollins.

Reutzel, D. & Cooter, R. (1996). *Teaching Children to Read From Basals to Books.* New Jersey: Merrill.

Roser, N.,97 Hoffman, J. & Farest, C. (1990). Language, Literature, and At-Risk Children. *The Reading Teacher*, 43 (8), pp. 554–561.

Simon, S. (1990). *New Questions and Answers About Dinosaurs.* New York: Morrow Junior Books.

Walmsley, S. & Walp, T. (1990). Integrating Literature and Composing into the Language Arts Curriculum: Philosphy and Practice. *The Elementary School Journal*, 90 (3), pp. 251–274.

Spotlight on **PRACTICE**

K a t h y   H a m m e r

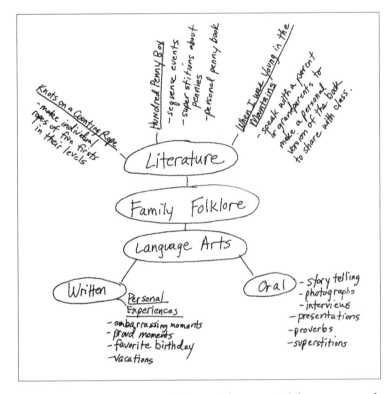

I have found that planning for a day in my classroom can be as shaky as a novice acrobat walking on a tightrope. There are always unexpected interruptions, changes in schedules, and other surprise occurrences. How do I work in as much of the curriculum as possible and give enough time to the wide range of subjects I'm expected to teach? I integrate curriculum areas into a central theme! When I plan, I spin a sort of web that can catch ideas to enrich and extend a lesson, a unit, or a piece of literature. The web enhances what is being studied, no matter what the subject area (such as science) or the content (such as magnets).

In this article I will focus on how I integrate reading, writing, listening, and speaking, with a special focus on reading activities. In practice, of course, all these areas emerge.

Philosophy

Reading (and the other elements of language arts) is important to me. I feel that students should be proficient in this area since the skill extends to other curriculum areas. Reading skills must come first, before the other subjects can be mastered. It is my goal to help my students to comprehend what they read, communicate in their own words what they've learned, and apply skills (such as using a dictionary or context clues) to maximize the information they receive. In many ways, I "teach" reading all day long, for it is a large part of all overall learning.

Webbing

Almost any book—from *Snakes* to *The Phantom Tollbooth*—can be used in ways that extend throughout the curriculum. Some books are better than others, but most can be extended into at least two other curriculum areas. I find the easiest way to plan for extending literature is by creating a web for the book. When I think about my curriculum and the skills my students are to master, I think about how I can tie those to an aspect of the book.

What is a web? For planning purposes, it is similar to an outline in that it helps to organize instruction. It is a way to brainstorm on paper. It does not have to be prepared in any specified format.

I've created webs on themes such as fall or nature or archaeology and on books such as *Moon of the Alligators* or *Artifacts from A to Z*. I place the theme in the center. Around that I write reading, writing, listening, speaking, and viewing. Within each section I jot down possible skills or concepts I want to incorporate in the unit. For example, for *Moon of the Alligators*, a unit I taught some time ago, I wrote under reading "discuss point of view." As ideas occur to me, I add them in the appropriate places.

Fortunately, there is no one right way to web. What fascinates me is that, as I list the areas I want to cover, I am able to view instantly how they may relate to another area of our district's curriculum. For example, if I've prepared a web on family folklore, I may see that by inviting grandparents in to tell family stories from the past (promoting students' listening skills), I'm also promoting students' interest in history.

More Advantages

Sometimes I ask my class to participate in the webbing of a new topic, rather than create a web on my own. This promotes student interaction and learning. On the board or on chart paper I write the theme and ask students to write their associations with that topic.

I recall my excitement one day as my class did a webbing on fall. I was using the web as a prewriting activity, to draw out students' thoughts about the season. I had given each student a large piece of paper. My instructions were to place the word *Fall* in the center, then jot down as many words and ideas about fall that they could think of.

Their crayons moved fast and furiously, filling their pages with words. When we regrouped to combine our thoughts and ideas on one large piece of butcher paper, hands flew up, one after another, as students offered their words and ideas.

When we began discussing leaves—their looks and sounds—one student said, "The leaves are like cats being chased by a big dog." That one comment inspired the others to think of similes, and their offerings became poetic phrases. One student summed up his thoughts about webbing with, "I think webbing is cool. You get to tell what you like to do and feel." When it was time to begin their writing project, they used both their individual webs as well as our large class web, and not one student had a difficult time with the assignment.

Use of Literature

I find that students learn skills more thoroughly when the skills are presented in conjunction with a piece of literature, rather than in an isolated lesson. With webbing, I have been able to make that happen. When webbing, all my students are able to participate. I find that their self-concepts are enhanced because their thoughts and ideas count ! Their learning, then, becomes more meaningful and is much more likely to be internalized and remembered. I feel that I am making sense out of learning.

My students have also begun to see the connectedness among the different subjects. One time I announced to my class that we were going to get ready to web about the forest. One little girl responded, "I like when we web! Webbing is a good way to think of stuff." My students don't just sit and listen to me. They sit and listen to other students and, most importantly, they *do*. They also learn to appreciate and respect the ideas of others. I have discovered that it is my students who set the pace, not I.

Strega Nona, by Tomie dePaola, is a wonderful book to read to and with children. Last year, as I planned for the unit, I created a web to see where and how I could extend the story to other areas of the curriculum. Before long, the ideas came to me. See the web that I created on this page. You will notice that by just using a fun, simple story, many important skills can be naturally incorporated in the lessons.

Involving students actively as learners helps make learning more meaningful. It also helps students remember. As they do things, children receive a better understanding of how the theme relates to concrete objects and ideas in their lives. With each passing year, I find that I rely less on textbooks, and more on the enormous amount of available literature in today's market.

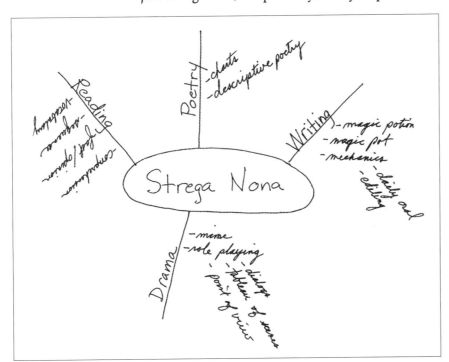

Teacher's Guides

Along with the many fine books for children, there are also hundreds of ready-made literature guides available for teachers. I have used many of them. I have learned, however, that on my own it is possible to create activities around a piece of literature, which specifically extends to areas of the curriculum that I am expected to cover.

Sometimes I use the guides as a springboard for other planning. When webbing, I pull in my resources from these guides, along with my own collection of professional books. The web I create provides me with a vision and direction for the unit.

Keep in mind: webs are never finished, and can be constantly updated, as need dictates. Creating a web for a book or poem takes no more of my time than writing plans in the planbook. But, for me and my students, webbing gives purpose to the unit and to our related activities.

Kathy Hammer teaches in the Chaney School in St. Louis, Missouri.

References

dePaola, T. (1979). *Strega Nona,* New York: Simon &Schuster.

George, J. C. (1991). *The Moon of the Alligators,* New York: HarperCollins.

Juster, N. (1988). *The Phantom Tollbooth,* New York: Knopf.

Moon, F. A. (1985). *Happy Birthday,* New York: Simon & Schuster,

Mathis, S. B. (19750), *Hundred-Penny Box,* New York: Viking,

Henkes, K. (1991). *Chrysanthemum,* New York: Greenwillow.

Martin, B., Jr., & Archambault, J. (1987). *Knots on a Counting Rope,* New York: H. Holt & Co.

Simon, S. (1992). *Snakes* New York: HarperCollins.

Assessing Your Classroom

Teachers who integrate language arts help their students learn concepts more effectively. Does your classroom show evidence of the following?

	Yes	Some	No
1 Writing			
Learning Logs			
Learning Webs			
Student Subject Area Journals			
Letters			
Poetry			
Commentaries			
Essays			
Computer Writing Activities			
Writing Center			
2 Reading Resources			
Books and stories written by children			
Fiction			
Nonfiction			
Periodicals, Newspapers, Magazines			
Reference Sources			
Children's Literature			
3 Speaking			
Oral Presentations/Demonstrations, Group Work			
Interviews			
Oral Histories			
Presentation of Research			
4 Listening Centers			
Books on Tape			
Homework on Tape			
Interviews			
Language Tapes			
5 Research and Critical Thinking			
Demonstration/Modeling			
Critical Thinking Activities			
Puzzles			
Mysteries			

Try This

(1) Reading, Writing, Speaking, Listening, Viewing
Choose a theme that helps your students create meaning from the selections they read. A theme will also help you tie together the different language arts experiences your students will have. For example, suppose you choose the theme of mysteries. You would then select several pieces of literature that reflect different aspects of the theme and which are likely to foster a lively interchange among your students. Identify the comprehension skills that flow from the selections, such as plot and problems and solutions. These are the skills that you will help your students master in this unit.

After reading and discussing the mystery, help your students gain hands-on experience in learning about and solving a mystery, by inviting them to reopen the case in the story. Have them work in small groups to brainstorm the kinds of questions a detective might ask. Tape-record detective-suspect interviews. Group members can take turns playing the different roles. After listening to the tape recordings, have the whole class decide on the solution.

You can also try a related writing activity that helps students learn about plot and problem/solution. Have students change a detail in the plot of the mystery to create a different outcome or solution. Talk with the class about what they learned.

(2) Writing
Use a writing activity to encourage further exploration of the mystery theme and genre. An interesting writing activity also provides a vehicle for the teaching of writing elements (plot and characterization, for example), along with grammar, usage, and mechanics. For example, you might call attention to a distinguishing feature of a mystery; that is, a mystery presents a puzzle to solve. Have students think about the different pieces of information given in the opening to the story. Talk about the ways in which these piece together to create a mystery to solve. Be sure to discuss related grammar, usage, and mechanics skills. Then have students write their own opening for a mystery, setting up a puzzle to solve. Discuss what students learned from the project, and make modifications for the next class you teach.

(3) Challenge Students to Create Their Own Mystery Projects
Develop a special project to help students gain additional hands-on experience with mysteries and establish a real-life connection. For example, one such project would be to have students work in groups to think of an idea for a television mystery series. Then have them create a commercial to entice viewers to watch the series. Have the groups perform their commercials for the class.

(4) Evaluate the effectiveness of the project on your class's interests and skills in reading

5

Using Literature in Your Classroom

Spotlight on THEORY

Douglas K. Hartman

Selecting Materials

The materials that students read are the core of any literacy curriculum. Think for a moment about what *your* students read. They probably enjoy literature that makes them laugh, captures their interests, and relates to their lives. Now think about what you read to your students. You probably select literature that evokes imaginative responses and intriguing discussions. Good literature is the material of choice for a good literacy curriculum.

But does a steady diet of good literature represent a *balanced* literacy curriculum? To answer this question, consider for a moment how important a balanced diet is to good health. What would happen if your students ate only breads and cereals for every meal? For example: For breakfast? Only cereal (no milk). For lunch? Only bread (no peanut butter or jam). And for dinner? Only spaghetti (no meat sauce). While their stomachs wouldn't be empty, your students would still be eating an unbalanced diet. According to the United States Department of Agriculture Food Pyramid, to ensure good health we should consume a balanced menu of items from all food groups.

Varied Selections

Should the materials students "consume" in a literacy curriculum be varied? Yes. A balanced "diet" of materials makes for a healthy literacy curriculum. What materials do I think students should read in a balanced literacy curriculum? What are some effective ways to present those materials? And in what ways might we, as teachers, ask students to respond to the materials? The answers to these questions are a good indication of the health of the literacy curriculum in any classroom, school, and district.

Materials for the Curriculum

Variety of materials is the key to a healthy literacy curriculum. Certainly, great literature should be at the heart of the curriculum. Nothing "feeds" students' imaginations better or connects to their lives more deeply than great stories. Today great stories as well as information, images, and sounds are being communicated through other media. These forms of communication have become as compelling and engaging as great stories.

To take advantage of expanding communication modes, we need a broadened conception of what can be "read." Such a conception includes traditional *linguistic* reading materials (such as stories, poems, articles, and chapters), as well as more *semiotic* "reading" materials (such as film, music, paintings, photographs, and dance). In a broad sense, all of these materials—both linguistic and semiotic—can be decoded, comprehended, and responded to by students.

Two reasons for providing a balanced diet of materials in the literacy curriculum: It provides opportunities to see how conventions for meaning-making are used across linguistic and semiotic materials. For example, students can compare how well a literary device such as "flashback" is used across the mediums of literature, film, and storytelling, and they can compare and evaluate how the various mediums employ the device.

It also includes real-world materials that students will use in their adult lives. For example, an architect who is developing a building for a client will have to know how to "read" survey maps, computer-generated traffic flow simulations, interview transcripts with users of the building, 3-D computer-generated floor plan models, geological and atmospheric data diagrams and charts, and building regulation guides.

Effective Ways to Present Materials

In Sets

First, students can read materials in *sets* that are topically, conceptually, or thematically related. Because a story, poem, article, painting, or film rarely stands alone, students need to develop a mind-set early on that the reading of any material is enhanced when read in the context of other related materials.

For example, rather than read Perrault's *Cinderella* as an isolated story, students can read it in the context of one or more of the numerous other print and film versions. Some 700 print and 50 film versions are available, as well as dance, musical, and illustrated versions of the story. The reason for clustering materials in sets like this is to help students deepen their understanding of literature, film, art, music, and dance (that is, the humanities) by seeing how a story is refracted through various cultural, historical, and social lenses.

In Arranged Sets

The second way students can read the materials is in strategically *arranged sets*. While there are no hard and fast rules for arranging sets of materials, there are a number of useful ways to think about the underlying relationships among them. These underlying types of relationships fall into five categories: complementary, conflicting, controlling, synoptic, and dialogic. (For a list of suggested works, see Arranging Texts on page 52.)

Complementary materials enhance and support various aspects of a topic. Through the relationships among the materials, you can provide varied and repeated opportunities for students to see the multifaceted nature of the topic.

For example, the topic of "Number Sense" can be explored through a set of complementary texts that give a feel for large numbers: Wanda Gag's story *Millions of Cats*; an information book titled *How Much is a Million?*; an information article of the same title (Goins); an historical account of how large numbers developed in *The Story of Numbers*; and a book filled with one million dots (*One Million*) provide students with many opportunities to construct, reconstruct, and synthesize information from multiple sources.

Conflicting materials represent alternative and problematic perspectives on a topic. Through the relationships among the materials, you bring competing viewpoints to center stage for students. For example, the topic "What Really Happened in History?" can be explored through conflicting accounts of the death of General James Wolfe at the battle of Quebec in September 1759 during the French and Indian War. These may include the event as mentioned in a social studies textbook (Hirsh), as described in a children's periodical (Collins), as painted (by West), as discussed in trade books (Henty, Marrin, Ochoa), and as retold by an historian (Schama).

A *controlling* set occurs where one material is used to frame the reading of others. Through the relationships among the materials, you use a central piece of material as a strategic device or authoritative expression for opening up students' understandings of other materials. For example, the topic of "Needing to Belong" in MacLachlan's *Sarah Plain and Tall* can be used as the controlling lens through which to read such subsequent texts as David McCord's "This is My Rock" (Cole, 1984), "Sumer Is Icumen In" (Caldwell & Kendrick, 1984), and *Maniac Magee* (Spinelli, 1990).

Synoptic materials highlight variants and versions of a single story or event. Through the relationships among the materials, you emphasize to students how a story is refracted through social, cultural, and historical lenses. For example, the topic of "Diversity Around the World" can be explored through a set of synoptic texts that focus on how fairy tales like *Cinderella* are rendered across various cultures. Students can read the linguistic versions of *Yeh-shen* (Ai-ling) (China),

Princess Furball (Huck) (Germany), *Vasilisa the Beautiful* (Whitney) (Russia), *Moss Gown* (Hooks) (Southern United States), and *Mufaro's Beautiful Daughter* (Steptoe) (Africa). The semiotic texts of Rodgers and Hammerstein's *Cinderella* (1964) musical and dramatic production of the story and The Berlin Comic Opera's *Cinderella Ballet* (Bey & Gawlick) dance interpretation of the fairy tale can be used in combination with the various linguistic versions.

Finally, **dialogic** materials represent an ongoing interchange or "dialogue" on a topic. Through the relationships among the materials, you facilitate a textual "conversation" in which characters, people, themes, and events appear and reappear across the many materials students read. Maurice Sendak's trilogy—*Where the Wild Things Are*, *In the Night Kitchen*, and *Outside Over There* — provide an example where interactions around the topic of "Dealing with Hardship" are exchanged and reworked across the companion set of materials.

The reason for arranging materials in strategically designed sets like these is to help students learn the skills and strategies necessary for locating, sifting through, analyzing, interpreting, and evaluating information. They will be better able to communicate ideas and responses to different audiences for a variety of purposes. These skills and strategies will figure prominently in their lives as active citizens and productive workers in the century to come.

Ways Students Can Respond to Materials in a Balanced Literacy Curriculum

We can invite students to respond in a variety of ways. To evoke these varied responses, prompt your students with (1) questions: "What did you think of the story?" and (2) statements: "Tell us your thoughts about the main character." Both prompts can be used to encourage students to speak, write, or draw about whatever they are reading. They can express their feelings and thoughts on the material—whether it's a single story, a subset of materials, or the entire set of materials. By asking students how a story makes them feel or what they think of the ideas presented across the materials, you are: (1) asking them to make connections that matter to them, and (2) gathering information about students' knowledge and skills. This in turn can inform the direction of your daily teaching and the planning for tomorrow and next week.

A Useful Framework
Developing prompts that elicit a balance of response modes requires a framework that recognizes the range of material sources students can draw upon in constructing their responses. One such framework divides response prompts into three types: **intratextual, intertextual,** and **extratextual.**

Intratextual prompts focus students on responding to a single material source. Examples include prompts that focus on a single feature ("How does author Babbit use the setting in *Tuck Everlasting* to support and drive the actions of the character?") or can be inferred by connecting information from several sentences or paragraphs ("How do the author's views of the Civil War change from the beginning to the middle and to the end of the chapter?")

Intertextual prompts focus students on responding to two or more sources by connecting them in some way. Examples include prompts that ask students to compare information from several sources such as: "How are the problems in all three stories alike or different?" Prompts can help students use information from a source to understand other materials ("How does the short article on black holes help you think about the music we heard on time travel?").

Extratextual prompts focus students on responding to a single source or set of materials by relating it to their personal experiences and opinions. For example, prompts that direct students to think actively about what they know about the topic ("What do you know about the way cats behave?") or which ask students to compare their own ideas with those of a film director ("In what ways do you agree or disagree with the film's message?").

The primary reason for using a balance of these prompt types is so students will learn to respond to and think about materials from many perspectives. Knowing how to approach a source on its own terms, in relationship to other materials, or by comparing it with one's own thoughts, imbues students with the most robust learning tools of all—understanding and thoughtfulness.

Final Thoughts

In sum, balance, in my opinion, should be the operative force in guiding what students read, how they read it, and how they respond to what they read. Use great literature as the core, but include a rich variety of semiotic materials as well. Provide carefully arranged sets of materials, knowing that students need many and varied opportunities to manipulate information for personal, social, and intellectual purposes. And, finally, encourage students to respond in a wide variety of ways, so that they develop the powerful and far-ranging skills necessary for making sense of the ever-increasing information sources in our media-rich world.

Douglas K. Hartman is Associate Professor of Language and Literacy, University of Pittsburgh; Editorial Board of The Reading Teacher and the National Reading Conference's Yearbook.

Arranging Texts
Suggested Works

COMPLEMENTARY
Theme: Number Sense

Ga'g, W. (1963). *Millions of Cats*. New York: Coward, McCann & Geoghegan.

Goins, E. H. (1975). How Much Is a Million? *Cricket*. 2 (9), 20–21.

Hertzberg, H. (1970). *One Million*. New York: Gemini Smith.

Lauber, P. (1961). *The Story of Numbers*. New York: Random House.

Schwartz, D. M. (1985). *How Much Is a Million?* New York: Lothrop, Lee & Shepard.

CONFLICTING
Theme: What Really Happened in History?
(Example: General James Wolfe's death at Quebec)

Collins, J. R. (April 1991). The Capture of Quebec. *Cobblestone*. 38–43.

Henty, G. A. (1961). *With Wolfe in Canada: Winning of a Continent*. New York: Walker.

Hirsch, S. A. (1988). *The United States: Its History and Neighbors*. Orlando, Florida: Harcourt Brace Javanovich.

Marrin, A. (1987). *Struggle for a Continent: The French and Indian Wars*. New York: Atheneum.

Ochoa, G. (1990). *The Fall of Quebec and the French and Indian War*. Englewood Cliffs, New Jersey: Silver Burdett.

Schama, S. (1991). *Dead Certainties: Unwarranted Speculations*. New York: Knopf.

West, B. (1770). *The Death of Benjamin Wolfe*. Ottowa: National Gallery of Canada.

CONTROLLING
Theme: Needing to Belong

Caldwell, M. and Kendrick, W. (Eds.) (1984). *The Treasury of English Poetry*. New York: Doubleday.

Cole, J. ed. (1984). *A New Treasure of Children's Poetry: Old Favorites and New Discoveries*. New York: Doubleday.

MacLachlan, P. (1985). *Sarah Plain and Tall*. New York: Harper & Row.

Spinelli, J. (1990). *Maniac Magee*. Boston, Massachusetts: Little, Brown.

SYNOPTIC
Theme: Diversity Around the World

Ai-ling, L. (1982). *Yeh-shen*. New York: Philomel.

Bey, H., Gawlick, R, and The Berlin Comic Opera. (1986). *Cinderella Ballet*. Berlin: VIEW.

Hooks, W. (1987). *Moss Gown*. New York: Clarion.

Huck, C. (1989) *Princess Furball*. New York: Greenwillow.

Rodgers, R. and Hammerstein, O. (1964). *Cinderella*. New York: CBS/Fox Video.

Steptoe, J. (1987). *Mufaro's Beautiful Daughter*. New York: Lothrop, Lee & Shepard.

Whitney, T. (1970). *Vasilisa the Beautiful*. New York: Macmillan.

DIALOGIC
Theme: Dealing With Hardship

Sendak, M. (1963). *Where the Wild Things Are*. New York: Harper Trophy.

Sendak, M. (1970). *In the Night Kitchen*. New York: Harper & Row.

Sendak, M. (1981). *Outside Over There*. New York: Harper & Row.

Spotlight on **PRACTICE**

Carol Hicks

Welcome to Our Classroom

For the past 17 years I have been teaching language arts and Spanish in a magnet program in an urban school system. Our fifth-grade classroom functions as a workshop, filled with a variety of materials and lots of interaction. In our classroom talking, writing, drawing, and dramatizing, in all their forms, are valued and encouraged. Literacy portfolios and response journals serve as the basic tools from, and through which, all activity is generated and constructed.

In this article I will describe how I have worked at balancing the literacy curriculum in a classroom filled with highly charged social activity. I have tried to create a classroom where students read a variety of materials that are carefully arranged, and where students respond to those materials in many ways.

Complementary Materials

I believe that using a variety of materials does wonders to balance the "diet" of my fifth-grade readers. Because I firmly believe that literature is the foundation of literacy learning, I begin unit and workshop sessions with powerful print materials.

Over the years, I have linked literature and film in a number of ways. For example, after we finish reading *Tuck Everlasting*, I show the film. The film provides students with new ways to appreciate the book and the book provides a context for the viewing of the film. This generates many interesting and challenging discussions among my students. One centers on differences between the book and the movie. For example, in the print version of *Tuck Everlasting*, a frog is christened with a drop of eternal water. However, in the film the animal is a turtle, not a frog. In class recently, students noted that difference and talked about why the filmmaker made that change. They queried: Is a turtle easier to see on screen than a frog? They observed that perhaps it's easier to place a drop of water on a turtle since that animal is less mobile than a frog. Students offered lots of ideas and suggestions.

We also talked about the effect of that change on them as viewers. They responded to the questions: What associations do you have with a turtle? With a frog? If you were a filmmaker, which animal would you use, and why? What research would the filmmaker have had to make to film a turtle and keep the animal healthy? We discussed aspects that went far beyond the basic plot of the story.

While focusing on seemingly minor differences between the book and film, students came to understand the unique ways in which each medium lends itself to the use of special literary devices, plot types, and character roles.

The same was true of our reading and viewing *The Reluctant Dragon*. Both the book and the movie stimulated many imaginative activities in the class. In fact, a group of students were so inspired by the two versions that they created a third and performed their own play of the story. They added their own innovative twist to the central plot.

Lessons Learned

I have learned two lessons about using a variety of materials. One is that a variety of text types keeps students *very* interested in what they are reading. That variety produces spirited discussions and motivated working groups. My students love stories, and I believe the diversity of materials they have been exposed to has contributed to that passion.

The second lesson relates to the students in my class who are reluctant readers or less-able readers. The mix of source types enables those students to participate in ways that would not have been possible with a print-only "diet." Reluctant readers are as eager to learn "what comes next" as are their more able classmates. When we see the film, *all* the students take pleasure in sharing their disappointments and delights about the casting of characters, the selection of scene locations, and the addition or deletion of particular events. It is a rewarding sight.

Arranging the Materials

I try hard to present materials that are rich with connections and that have underlying relationships.

For many years I asked my students to read books in thematically related sets, such as books on Growing Up or Family Relationships. This was a success, but I learned that sets of materials also need to be carefully arranged. As I experimented with various arrangements and combinations, my planning and teaching changed in ways that dramatically helped my students. They were better able to learn to analyze, synthesize, and evaluate information across materials in much more complex and interesting ways.

The School Year Begins

I begin the school year by framing the entire year's reading around the book *The Trumpet of the Swan*. This story serves as the controlling lens through which my fifth-graders' view all other materials.

We Read On

The second book I present is one that conflicts, in rather dramatic ways, with the first. For example, this year I followed *The Trumpet of the Swan* with *Tuck Everlasting*. My students wondered long and hard about important ways this second book differed from the first. One student said that the theme of *The Trumpet of the Swan* is "knowing life through death." Another student added that *Tuck Everlasting* focuses on the pain of a "life without death" in order to "give life meaning." In discussing the differences between the two works, my students engaged in critical analysis and higher-level thinking.

Fairy Tales Serve Purpose

I like to break up the reading and viewing of long works by introducing short selections in between. The most common type of segue I use is the fairy tale. We usually spend about one week on each story.

The fairy tale serves a number of purposes.

- It offers a quick set of short reading encounters.

- It serves as a topical transition between the long literary works.

- It provides reinforcement for the ideas and themes that appear and reappear throughout the year.

One recent week of fairy-tale reading focused on *Cinderella* stories. The theme of the respectful, yet independent girl in these tales served as a natural bridge between the character Louis in the *Trumpet of the Swan* and the character Winnie in *Tuck Everlasting*. As is typical, the *Cinderella* stories spilled over into other curriculum areas, such as Spanish class, where I used the story as part of language acquisition activities.

More Lessons Learned

From having stitched, unstitched, and restitched materials in many curricular patterns over the years, I have learned two things.

1. **Think carefully about how to arrange materials.** I try not to throw together a set that is convenient or looks sensible on the surface. With hindsight I see that my acquisition and use of deep underlying relations

among materials provides a rich curriculum for my students to learn and respond in ways that go beyond surface strategies.

2. **Take the long view when using carefully arranged materials.** I start out small and work toward creating an ideal unit over a number of years.

Responding to the Materials

Responding to materials is an important part of my program. How do I encourage student responses? I use two basic strategies: I provide spaces for responses and use multileveled prompts to evoke student responses.

Provide Room

I designate three response locations within the classroom.

- *Response journal area*—a writing and drawing space—where students, the teacher, and parents interact around ideas presented in the materials.

- *Discussion area*—a speaking space—where our conversations grow out of and feed into the response journals and other materials.

- *Stage area*—a dramatic space—at one end of the classroom where students can move to act out a scene or idea, or compose a play or skit.

Students respond to materials during and after every reading event. My goal is for response to become part of a basic interaction with texts of all types. Recently, my students started keeping "buddy journals," in which they write comments to another classmate whom they choose. At times, I write in their journals, too. It's quite exciting! I find that by creating response triangles I am able to encourage reluctant writers.

Together, these three response locations provide my students with the linguistic and semiotic spaces necessary to respond to materials in a variety of ways.

Use Multileveled Questions

The other strategy is to use prompts that evoke student responses at a number of levels. Most often, I begin with intratextual prompts, move on to extratextual prompts, and then expand to intertextual prompts. Intertextual prompts engage students in especially thoughtful responses.

For example, after discussing E. B. White's *The Trumpet of the Swan* and *Charlotte's Web*, I ask my students to write about what they have learned about White from his works. By recollecting snippets from their previous journal entries, drawings, conversations, and dramatic exercises, students sketch a profile of an author who has deep respect for nature and the life cycle, and who portrays a world where life, death, and seasonal changes are all part of the world's beauty.

Carol M. Hicks is a teacher in the Liberty Elementary School in the Pittsburgh Public Schools.

References

Babbitt, N. (1975). *Tuck Everlasting*. New York: Farrar, Straus, & Giroux.

David M. S.(1985). *How Much is a Million?* New York: Lothrop, Lee & Shepard.

Gag, W. (1977). *Millions of Cats*. New York: Putnam.

Grahame, K. (1983). *The Reluctant Dragon*. New York: H. Holt & Co.

Hertzberg, H. (1993). *One Million*. New York: Random House.

Hooks, W. H. (1987). *Moss Gown*. Boston, Massachusetts: Houghton Mifflin.

Huck, C. (1989). *Princess Furball*. New York: Greenwillow.

Lauber, P. (1961). *The Story of Numbers*. New York: Random House.

Louie, Al-Ling (1990). *Yeh Shen: A Cinderella Story from China*. New York: Putnam.

MacLachlan, P. (1985). *Sarah, Plain & Tall*. New York: HarperCollins.

Perrault, C. (1985). *Cinderella*. New York: Dial Books for Young Readers.

Sendak, M. (1970). *In the Night Kitchen*. New York: HarperCollins.

Sendak, M. (1981). *Outside Over There*. New York: HarperCollins.

Sendak, M. (1988). *Where the Wild Things Are*. New York: HarperCollins.

Spinelli, J. (1990). *Maniac Magee*. New York: Little, Brown & Co.

Steptoe, J. (1987). *Mufaro's Beautiful Daughters: An African Tale*. New York: Lothrop, Lee & Shepard.

White, E.B. (1952). *Charlotte's Web*. New York: HarperCollins.

White, E.B. (1970). *The Trumpet of the Swan*. New York: HarperCollins.

Winthrop, E. (1994). *Vasilissa the Beautiful*. New York: HarperCollins.

Assessing Your Classroom

Use the following checklist to reflect on and evaluate the types of materials available in your literacy curriculum, the ways the materials are arranged, and the ways in which students respond to the materials.

1 Types of Materials

- Are students reading a variety of materials?
- Across the school year, what percentage of the materials are:

    linguistic? (stories, poems, articles, chapters) _____%

    semiotic? (films, music, paintings, photographs, dance) _____%

2 Arrangement of Materials

- Are students reading materials in sets that are topically, conceptually, or thematically related?
- Have you strategically arranged the materials so that they are rich with many potential connections to each other and the topic?
- Are the materials organized so that their underlying relationships can be recognized by students?

3 Response to Materials

- Do you provide response space in the classroom for students to:

    write?

    draw?

    talk?

    act?

- Do you prompt students to respond to a source:

    on its own terms? (intratextual)

    in terms of other materials? (intertextual)

    in terms of their own thoughts? (extratextual)

Try This

(1) Take a photograph, object, or any artifact and practice "reading" it.

Learning to "read" semiotic materials (such as film, music, paintings, photographs, and dance) is often a new experience for students. To introduce the idea in a fun way, begin by having students closely observe an old photo, a baseball bat, or a worn-out pair of tennis shoes. Ask students two questions, and offer plenty of think-time and support of their reactions:

- What do you see?
- What does it mean?

As students note carefully what they see in the artifacts and then speculate on what their observations might mean, they get a better sense of what it's like to "read" semiotic materials.

(2) Visit the library to find a number of books, articles, films, paintings, and songs related to a topic or theme of interest to you. Sketch out possible ways to arrange the material for use with your students.

Locating materials is often a time-consuming task, and arranging them into sets is often a challenging exercise. But it is well worth the investment of your time and effort.

(3) Have students read two or more sources and practice connecting them.

Give students practice in responding to two or more materials (intertextual prompt). To introduce the strategy and encourage intellectual risk taking, have students play a game called The Web.

In The Web small teams of students search for as many connections as they can find among several source materials within a given time period. One person in each group records the connections that are proposed. Songs, pictures, poems, TV commercials, and objects are good materials that lend themselves well to this high-energy, action-packed thinking game.

6

Teaching Skills and Strategies with Literature

Spotlight on THEORY

James F. Baumann

Helene Hooten

Patricia White

Direct instruction [in reading skills and strategies] is neither a panacea nor a curse. It simply represents one additional tool that has its place in a balanced reading and language arts instructional program. Like most other educational methodologies, direct instruction should be used wisely, discriminatingly, and in moderation. (Baumann, 1988, p. 717)

The heart of a powerful reading program is the relationship between explicit, systematic skills instruction and literature, language, and comprehension. While skills alone are insufficient to develop good readers, no reader can become proficient without these foundational skills. (*Every Child a Reader*, 1995, p. 3)

In order for students to become skilled, fluent, lifelong readers, they need to possess an interest in books, a desire to read, and the ability to read and comprehend written text. In other words, students need both the will and the skill to use reading for learning, enjoyment, and personal fulfillment. The challenge for classroom teachers is to achieve a delicate balance between enticing students to explore literature and providing youngsters with the ability to read and respond to printed material.

In this chapter, we present a rationale for integrating the teaching of reading skills and strategies with literature and summarize an instructional program we implemented in Helene's and Pat's fifth-grade classrooms over an entire school year (Baumann, White, & Hooten, 1994). In our companion chapter, we describe in detail the literature-based strategy lessons we created and taught.

Defining Terms

Literature-based reading instruction is the teaching of reading and language arts abilities through the use of authentic reading materials—primarily trade books—written for children and young adults. Important objectives of this approach are (1) the growth of students' knowledge and appreciation of literature and (2) development of students as skillful, strategic readers. Literature-based instruction can be based on a program that involves the use of trade books exclusively (Cox & Zarillo, 1993; Routman, 1991; Tompkins & McGee, 1993), or it can combine the integrated use of a basal anthology with trade books (Wepner & Feeley, 1993). However, central to all literature-based programs is the importance of having students spend considerable amounts of time reading and responding to quality literature.

We define reading skills and strategies as abilities language users employ intentionally, selectively, and flexibly for the purpose of decoding, comprehending, or responding to written text (Baumann, 1991). Examples of reading strategies are:

- a reader using context clues to infer the meaning of an unknown word that is central to the comprehension of a passage;

- a reader looking for main ideas and topic sentences while trying to extract the important ideas from a challenging science textbook selection;

- a reader calling up knowledge of the characteristics of historical fiction in order to understand and enjoy a narrative text.

A critical feature of a balanced literature-based program is to provide skill instruction that is explicit and efficient (Baumann, 1988). Strategies selected for instruction should be high-utility abilities that students can use in multiple contexts, for example, using comprehension fix-up strategies such as rereading or paraphrasing when the meaning of a passage is unclear. In addition, instruction should be succinct, so that students spend the majority of time reading, responding to, or learning from texts. Finally, skill instruction should be integrated into the context of literary and informational texts, with teachers showing students how skills function and can be useful within typical reading situations.

Theoretical Background

Many writers have described the power and appropriateness of employing a literature-based perspective for teaching reading (Cullinan, 1987, 1992). In addition, there is evidence of a significant trend toward the implementation of literature-based programs in K–8 schools across the United States in various forms (Hiebert & Colt, 1989; Walmsley, 1992).

Most fully articulated literature-based approaches account for instruction in reading skills or strategies balanced with immersing students in literature (Tompkins & McGee, 1993). Some writers, however, have expressed concern with the limited attention given to reading skills or strategies in literature-based and other holistic approaches to reading. They argue that immersion in literature alone is insufficient; instead, students need to be taught directly how to perform language tasks (Spiegel, 1992).

A Yearlong Investigation

Research linking a literature-based perspective with explicit, teacher-led instruction is limited (Collins, 1993). Therefore, we conducted a study to explore this issue in depth (Baumann et al., 1994). We emphasized reading comprehension strategies in our program because most of the fifth-graders in Helene's and Pat's classes had adequately developed decoding skills. However, instruction in word identification strategies can be integrated within a literature-based framework just as effectively (Baumann, 1995).

Within our program, we taught a variety of comprehension strategies that included:

- using prediction and verification to anticipate and confirm ideas in the text;

- retelling and asking questions to clarify confusing or difficult texts;

- using story structure to understand narratives;

- writing about literature to explore meaning;

- learning about literary genres to have frameworks for comprehending a variety of textual forms.

Students read high-quality trade books that presented preadolescents in multiple roles. For example, the fifth-graders read humorous works (such as *The 18th Emergency*, Byars, 1973) and factually-based narratives (such as *Man From the Sky*, Avi, 1980). We also selected titles that reflected the diversity of the students in Pat's and Helene's classrooms (Harris, 1992), including realistic fiction (for example, *Yellow Bird and Me*, Hansen, 1986) and nonfiction (for example, *One More River to Cross: The Stories of Twelve Black Americans*, Haskins, 1992).

Strategy Lessons

We taught three different types of reading strategy lessons in conjunction with literature:

- *Elaborated* strategy lessons were teacher-directed lessons through which we introduced a skill or strategy. We explained the strategy, modeled it, and provided guided and independent practice, all within a meaningful story context.

- *Brief* strategy lessons were typically review or extension lessons. We revisited a previously taught strategy and provided reinforcement.

- *Mini* strategy lessons were unplanned (Durkin, 1990). We seized an instructional opportunity by engaging in an on-the-spot lesson that flowed from the reading or discussion of a selection.

The results of our program were positive (Baumann et al., 1994). The students learned the strategies and skills well, applying them to the books used to teach the skills. They transferred their knowledge by using the strategies when reading subsequent titles. Further, our data challenged the suggestion that incorporating skill instruction with literature will inhibit students' aesthetic response or enjoyment of reading (Cox & Zarillo, 1993). In fact, as the year progressed, the students read much more than in the past while exhibiting improved attitudes toward reading and literature.

Note: The research and development effort described in this and the next chapter was supported by the National Reading Research Center of the University of Georgia and the University of Maryland under the Educational Research and Development Centers Program (PR/AWARD NO. 117A20007) as administered by the Office of Educational Research and Improvement, U.S. Department of Education. The findings and opinions expressed here do not necessarily reflect the position or policies of the National Reading Research Center, the Office of Educational Research and Improvement, or the U.S. Department of Education.

James F. Baumann is a Professor of Reading Education at the University of Georgia. Helene Hooten and Patricia White are fifth grade teachers at Gaines Elementary School in Athens, Georgia.

References

Avi. (1980). *Man from the Sky.* New York: Morrow.

Baumann, J. F. (1988). Direct Instruction Reconsidered. *Journal of Reading, 31,* 712–718.

Baumann, J. F. (1991). Of Rats and Pigeons Skills and Whole Language. *Reading Psychology, 12,* iii–xiii.

Baumann, J. F. (1995, September). 180 Days in Second Grade Growing and Knowing Together. *NRRC News A Newsletter of the National Reading Research Center,* 1–3.

Baumann, J. F., White, P., & Hooten, H. (1994, May). Teaching Comprehension Strategies with Trade Books: A Collaborative Study in Two Fifth-Grade Classrooms. Research report presented at Reading Research '94, a meeting sponsored by the International Reading Association and the major literacy centers, Toronto, Canada.

Byars, B. (1973). *The 18th Emergency.* New York: Viking.

Collins, C. C. (1993). Strategy Instruction in a Literature-Based Reading Program. *The Elementary School Journal*, 94, 139–151.

Cox, C. & Zarillo, J. (1993). *Teaching Reading with Children's Literature*. New York: Macmillan.

Cullinan, B. E. (Ed.). (1987). *Children's Literature in the Reading Program*. Newark, Delaware: International Reading Association.

Cullinan, B. E. (Ed.). (1992). *Invitation to Read More Children's Literature in the Reading Program*. Newark, Delaware: International Reading Association.

Durkin, D. D. (1990). Dolores Durkin Speaks on Instruction. *The Reading Teacher*, 43, 472–476.

Every Child a Reader. (1995). The Report of the California Reading Task Force. Sacramento: California Department of Education.

Hansen, J. (1986). *Yellow Bird and Me*. New York: Clarion.

Harris, V. (Ed.). (1992). *Teaching Multicultural Literature in Grades K–8*. Norwood, Massachusetts: Christopher-Gordon.

Haskins, J. (1992). *One More River to Cross: The Stories of Twelve Black Americans*. New York: Scholastic.

Hiebert, E. H. & Colt, J. (1989). Patterns of Literature-Based Reading Instruction. *The Reading Teacher*, 43, 14–20.

Routman, R. (1991). *Invitations: Changing as Teachers and Learners*. Portsmouth, New Hampshire: Heinemann.

Spiegel, D. L. (1992). Blending Whole Language and Direct Instruction. *The Reading Teacher*, 46, 38–44.

Tompkins, G. E. & McGee, L. M. (1993). *Teaching Reading with Literature: Case Studies to Action Plans*. New York: Macmillan.

Walmsley, S. A. (1992). Reflections on the State of Elementary Literature Instruction. *Language Arts*, 69, 508–514.

Wepner, S. B. & Feeley, J. T. (1993). *Moving Forward with Literature Basals, Books, and Beyond*. New York: Macmillan.

Yopp, R. H. & Yopp, H. K. (1992). *Literature-Based Reading Activities*. Needham Heights, Massachusetts: Allyn & Bacon.

Spotlight on **PRACTICE**

James F. Baumann

Helene Hooten

Patricia White

Described here are the three types of literature-based reading strategy lessons we described briefly in the preceding section; that is, *elaborated, brief,* and *mini-lessons.* We introduce many of our lessons with the help of a fictional character: Clark Canine Super Reporter (Baumann, Jones, & Seifert-Kessell, 1993), a kind of Superman character who "helps" us teach comprehension skills (see Box 6.1). Through a series of lessons, we use Clark Canine to show that readers interact with text in ways similar to those that reporters use to interact with people. We teach students to monitor their comprehension and employ various fix-up strategies with Clark's help. Examples of each type of strategy lesson follow.

Box 6.1: **Clark Canine Super Reporter's Instructional Chart**

REPORTERS	**READERS**
• *Interview* people by asking questions.	• *Interview* writers by asking questions.
• *Retell* what the person said.	• *Retell* what the writer wrote.
• *Write* ideas from the interview.	• *Write* ideas about the story.
• Put *important ideas* in the story.	• Put *important ideas* in their memory.
• *Predict* what people will say.	• *Predict* what writers will write.
• Make sure they *get* all the story.	• *Map* the story in their minds.

Elaborated Strategy Lesson: Predicting and Verifying

One of the first strategies we teach is how to make predictions and how to verify or change those predictions as students read on in a story. We have taught this strategy as an elaborated lesson in conjunction with the reading of *Man From the Sky* (Avi, 1980). *Man From the Sky* is the story of Jamie, an eleven-year-old boy, who sees a criminal parachuting from an airplane. The boy becomes entangled with the criminal's attempted escape. We selected this title because it was engaging and suspenseful, qualities that made the book well suited to teaching predicting.

We begin by discussing what a prediction is (students have responded "predicting the weather," "betting on a game"). Then we present a read-predict-check-change strategy (*see* Box 6.2). As the children flip through the pages of the book and look at the table of contents, they offer predictions about the story. We list the predictions on the board and return to them later. Students evaluate predictions by writing "T" ("True") for predictions that were proved correct in the text, "F" ("False") for predictions disconfirmed by the text, and "CT" ("Can't Tell") when the text did not enable the reader to confirm or refute the prediction. Box 6.3 shows predictions students made about *Man From the Sky* and their evaluations of them. (Some predictions changed from "CT" to "T" or "F" as they read on in the book.)

Box 6.2: How to Make Predictions

1. **Read** part of the story.

2. **Predict** what will happen next.

3. Read on and then **Check** your predictions.

4. **Change** or **Make New** predictions.

Box 6.3: Students' Group Predictions
Predictions for Avi's Man From the Sky

- I predict that Jamie will learn how to read. (CT → T)

- I think that Jamie will see Goddard parachute from the sky and catch him. (first part T; second part CT → T)

- I think Goddard will try to capture Jamie or Gillian. (CT → T)

- Grandma and Grandpa won't believe Jamie if he says he saw a parachutist. (CT → T)

- Gillian will want to know why Jamie is always looking at the sky. (T)

- Jamie will tell on Goddard, who will get caught, and the Luries will not tease Jamie anymore. (CT → T)

- Goddard will drop the bag. (T)

- He will make it to Elmira. (CT → F)

- Gillian will find the money and keep it. Goddard will come after her. (T)

- Gillian will become a cloud watcher, too. (T)

- People will start to believe Jamie. (T)

- Jamie will become a hero (he'll tell on Goddard; Goddard will get caught; Jamie will get a reward). (T, but CT for reward bit)

- Jamie might get some of the million dollars. (CT)

- Jamie's grandparents will worry if Gillian and Jamie get caught. (T)

Melissa   October 11
CT ① I think that Jamie will see Ed Goddard jump out of the plane

T ② I think Ed Goddard is a bad guy.

CT ③ I think that Jamie's sky watching will get him into trouble.

Wow! Interesting predictions! You've really got the hang of it! ☺

Throughout the school year, students also keep dialogue journals in which they write responses to the books. (We respond to their entries periodically.) They use the journals to apply the strategies they've learned. For example, we ask students to read several chapters from *Man From the Sky* independently and then write predictions. After reading several more chapters, we ask students to return to their predictions and evaluate them in writing. Box 6.4 shows some of Melissa's predictions for *Man From the Sky*. The final comment is one Jim wrote after reading Melissa's predictions.

Brief Strategy Lesson: Retelling

In this strategy lesson, we review and provide guided practice in the use of retelling. Retelling helps students understand and clarify the meaning of a text. (The lesson was taught in its elaborated form the preceding day.) We use *Yellow Bird and Me* (Hansen, 1986) to help teach retelling. *Yellow Bird and Me* is the story of Doris, a serious adolescent who befriends Yellow Bird, who is the class clown. Yellow Bird acts out as a way to cover his reading/learning problems. A sequel to *The Gift-Giver* (Hansen, 1980), *Yellow Bird and Me* presents urban, African-American preteens in sensitive, realistic, and sometimes humorous situations. The students have already read and discussed the first two chapters in *Yellow Bird and Me*.

We begin by reviewing the purpose of the retelling strategy using a teaching chart (see Box 6.5). Next, we model the strategy by retelling aloud the first chapter of the book. Then as an application activity, we ask the students to meet with partners to retell Chapter 2. Later, we meet as a group to discuss successes and frustrations with the strategy.

We have found that students demonstrate

Box 6.5 Retelling Instructional Chart
To RETELL part of a story, try. . .

- Putting the story into your own words.

- Saying the ideas in the order they happened in the story.

- Including all the most important events and ideas.

- Using the book to help you remember events or ideas.

spontaneous use of strategies. For example, when we asked students to write an open-ended response in their journals, Michael—on his own—chose to write a chapter-by-chapter synopsis, a form of written retelling (see Box 6.6). Antoine wrote a concise summary, another form of retelling (see Box 6.7).

Box 6.6: Spontaneous Chapter-by-Chapter Retelling of *Yellow Bird*

Chapter 1 is about Doris is trying to write a poem but Yellow Bird is distracting her. She helps Yellow Bird with Social Studies and goes on.
Then on Chapter 2 she continues to write the poem then when Mickey bothers her Doris gots in trouble. Bird blurts the correct awnsers that Doris was for Social Studies Then, she dropped the note and Mrs. Barker got the note, but Bird said it was his. Then the poem got around the room. When people teased, especially Mickey, Dotty, and Lavinia, Doris was mad at Yellow Bird.

Dear Michael,
You have written an excellent summary of the important ideas in chapters 1 and 2. Way to go! I'm even more impressed with your opinions I'm glad you like this book. Why do you like it so far? Why are you recommending it to other kids? Please write back.
M. B. 11-4

Opinions I like this book. I could recommend this book for people who love reading. I think Doris and Yellow Bird are good characters This book has a very good plot.

Box 6.7: Synopsis of Section of *Yellow Bird*

Dear, Journal
Yellow Bird is a sly person in the store. Doris doesn't like the twins and Yellow Bird. Yellow Bird needs help with he's work and reading skils because he can't read to good. Doris doesn't like Yellow Bird because he took the letter that Doris's wrote to Amir. Everybody was giggleing at Doris

Dear Antoine,
You have written some excellent ideas Antoine. Very fine work! How do you think Doris is feeling now? How would you feel? What about Yellow Bird? What do you think will happen to him? Keep up the good work, and please write back!
M. B
11/4

Mini Strategy Lesson: Characterization

While reading the realistic fiction book *The 18th Emergency* (Byars, 1973), our group held an unexpected discussion of character traits. *The 18th Emergency* is about Mouse Fawley, a likable but eccentric twelve-year-old who imagines various emergencies and escape procedures, but ends up dealing with a real-life emergency after he insults the vengeful school bully. While discussing the opening chapters of this book, the students began to describe Mouse, using words such as *coward*, *weird*, *clever*, and *imaginative*. We quickly conducted an impromptu lesson on characterization, a strategy we had planned on introducing later in the term.

During the lesson, we created a character map of Mouse and discussed how authors use words to paint pictures of characters. Based on this on-the-spot lesson, we then planned and conducted an elaborated lesson on characterization on the following day. This led us to create maps of various story characters (Box 6.8) and write journal entries that focus on character traits (Box 6.9).

Box 6.8: **Cicely's Map of Ezzie, Mouse's Friend**

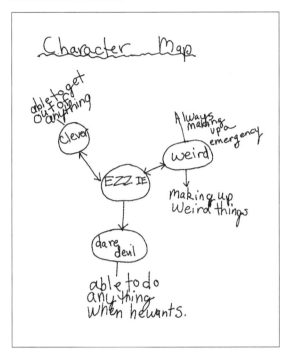

Box 6.9: **Journal Entry Focused on Character Traits**

Thanks for writing back. I wanna know why does mouse have to be so afraid of Marv. I think marv is really a scardy cat. If I were mouse, I would give him, lift hook, then a right one. Some uppercutts and some jabs.

5-2

Cory,

Well, I guess Marv wasn't so afraid after all (he did fight with Mouse). But Hammerman seemed to have a heart after, don't you think?

m.B.

Conclusion

B y taking the time to plan and implement systematic and impromptu mini strategy lessons, we saw students grow both in their ability to understand text and in their appreciation of quality literature (Baumann, White, & Hooten, 1994). For example, Sheena found and read *The Gift-Giver*. Then in her journal she predicted what events might follow *Yellow Bird* and concluded with "Joyce Hansen ought to write another book about them [characters in *Yellow Bird*]." Cicely had a similar journal response: "I really love this book *Yellow Bird and Me*. I want to read *The Gift-Giver*." Then after summarizing the ending of *Yellow Bird and Me*, Cicley asked, "Do you know where I can find this book? I would like to have one of my own." These representative responses told us that our program was successful in achieving both our goals of helping students develop the skill and the will to read. And, yes, we privately bequeathed to Cicely a copy of *Yellow Bird and Me*.

James F. Baumann is Professor of Reading Education at the University of Georgia.
Helene Hooten and Patricia White are fifth-grade teachers at Gaines Elementary School in Athens, Georgia.

References

Avi. (1980). *Man From the Sky*. New York: Morrow.

Baumann, J. F., Jones, L., & Seifert-Kessell, N. (1993). Using Think Alouds to Enhance Children's Comprehension Monitoring Abilities. *The Reading Teacher*, 47, 184–193.

Baumann, J. F., White, P., & Hooten, H. (1994, May). Teaching Comprehension Strategies with Trade Books: A Collaborative Study in Two Fifth-Grade Classrooms. Research report presented at Reading Research '94, a meeting sponsored by the International Reading Association and the major literacy research centers, Toronto, Canada.

Byars, B. (1973). *The 18th Emergency*. New York: Viking.

Hansen, J. (1980). *The Gift-Giver*. Boston: Houghton Mifflin.

Hansen, J. (1986). *Yellow Bird and Me*. New York: Clarion.

Assessing Your Classroom

Creating a strategy-based literature program involves the orchestration of many variables. To help you evaluate your movement toward this objective, try asking and answering the following questions about your evolving program:

	Yes	Some	No
Materials			
• Do I have a suitable classroom library of children's and young adult trade books?			
• Do I have access to multiple copies of some trade titles for group common readings?			
• Do I have a cooperative relationship with the school library media specialist, so that my students and I have regular access to the collection?			
• Is there a quality literature anthology available to me for integrating skill instruction with literature?			
• Am I ensuring that my students have access to books that represent multiple genres, involve classic and contemporary works, represent the diversity across the world community, and are authored by established and rising authors?			
Strategies			
• Am I teaching high-utility strategies?			
• Are the strategies linked well to the books and reading selections?			
• Am I including strategies that are appropriate for both fiction and nonfiction texts?			
• Does my instruction include comprehension monitoring and fix-up strategies?			
Instruction			
• Am I using a verbal explanation, modeling, guided practice, independent practice, instructional sequence?			
• Do I draw instructional examples from the texts we are reading?			
• Are we applying strategies in subsequent reading?			
• Do we come back and review previously taught strategies in new contexts?			
• Do I seize the instructional moment and teach mini strategy lessons?			
• Am I using analogies, metaphors, and concrete examples to help my students grasp the strategies I am teaching?			
Ambiance			
• Are the students and myself enjoying the literature we are reading?			
• Does my strategy-based reading program help students develop both the skill and the will to read?			
• Are my students feeling successful and becoming more motivated to read for learning and enjoyment?			

Try This

1 Focus on high-utility skills and strategies.

Select high-utility, transferable skills and strategies. We have found the following strategies to be useful across multiple texts and tasks:

Predicting and verifying—projecting what might happen in a selection, reading to evaluate projections, and then confirming, modifying, or making new predictions.

Inferring unstated ideas—teaching a generalized "what the author didn't tell you" strategy, for example, inferring setting information, character motives and actions, and an author's point of view.

Important information—learning that there are central elements in a narrative (the "story map" idea) and main ideas in informational texts (broad topics, section and paragraph main ideas).

Comprehension monitoring—learning to ask "Does this make sense?" and then having a repertoire of fix-up strategies when the answer is "no" rereading, paraphrasing, retelling, reading on and withholding judgment, and discussing a selection with fellow students.

2 Try a new instructional sequence.

We have found it useful to structure lessons according to the following steps:

Verbal Explanation—describe strategy you will teach, explain why it will help students become more skillful readers, and discuss how the strategy works.

Modeling—demonstrate how a skill or strategy functions, drawing from the trade book you are reading.

Guided Practice—allow students to try out the strategy themselves as they read a book, while you are present to provide more examples, reteaching, and reinforcement.

Independent Practice—give students a chance to try out a strategy as they read independently.

3 Match strategies to the books you select.

Teach strategies that are applicable to the texts you are reading. For example, you might teach the genre of historical fiction with Lois Lowry's *Number the Stars*. Conversely, you might teach the use of context clues to determine the meanings of unfamiliar or technical words in the nonfiction book, *Come Back, Salmon*.

4 Keep a balance between strategy instruction and literary experiences.

Our 80 to 20 percent ratio between time spent reading, discussing, and responding to literature versus time devoted to strategy instruction worked well for us. You, too, should find a comfortable division between literary tasks and the teaching of reading skills and strategies. Don't lose sight of the forest (developing responsive, engaged, motivated readers) for the trees (teaching students the skills necessary to achieve the preceding).

5 Enjoy what you are doing.

A strategy-based literature program provides your students opportunities to read quality literature while developing expertise as readers. Have fun along with your students as you explore the exciting and rewarding world of children's and young-adult's books.

The Role of Mentors and Apprentices

Spotlight on **THEORY**

David Rose

If you're like me, you can still remember how you learned to ride a bike. I can remember being perched on the seat of my sister's bike, pointing down the lawn toward the driveway. My father firmly held me and the bike upright as he began to gently push me forward. At first he did everything. He provided the power while my feet dangled limply over the pedals. He steered the bike as my hands gripped the handlebars in terror. He provided the balance, and I leaned into his shoulder. Gradually, over a number of "runs," he released his support—first the handlebars, then the seat, then the running alongside. Finally, I was riding alone, or almost. Ten yards later, I fell, but now I knew what to do, and I knew I could do it. Soon enough I was going way too far from home. My apprenticeship was quickly over.

The approach to teaching my dad took is as old as culture itself, and as modern as cognitive science. When people set out to teach new skills—how to "do" something—they often adopt apprentice models, either formally or informally. Conversely, whenever people learn how to do new things, whether it is learning to read, ride a bike, or build a nuclear reactor, they usually learn by becoming apprentices.

Apprentice learning is a fundamental part of real life. In this article I will discuss the importance of this kind of learning and explain its effective role in school.

The Elements of Apprenticeship

The elements of apprenticeship learning are simple.

1. First, there is usually a mentor who is already skillful in the domain—

someone who knows how to ride a bike, for example—and who can show others how its done. The mentor's role is to provide support when needed, and to draw the learner's attention selectively to important facets of the skill. "Watch how I use the pedals." "Watch how I lean when I turn." "Observe how I figure out the meaning of this word."

2. Apprenticeship offers opportunity for guided practice. No one can learn to ride a bike by watching someone else do it, or by hearing about it in a lecture. Skills are developed through active, meaningful practice. Every bike rider, like every reader, has practiced a great deal.

3. Often scaffolds support the apprentice. These scaffolds ensure that learners engage in meaningful tasks with successful results right from the beginning. For the apprentice bike rider, scaffolds might be training wheels or a mentor who runs along holding the bike up. For the emergent reader, the scaffold might be illustrations that support a text or a mentor who offers encouragement and models the task in clear, easy steps.

4. These scaffolds are faded or "gradually released" so that performance is more and more independent as skills develop. In my father's case, he began holding the bike and me with both hands. In time, he let go of one hand, then (and I remember this clearly because I did the same with my daughter) let go of everything but one finger with which he psychologically held me firm against the malevolent power of gravity. Finally, he ran alongside with "no fingers." This gradual release of support had an important effect—from the beginning I was performing the full act of riding the bike. I was performing an authentic task and having fun. Beginning readers need this same power, from attempting an authentic task with support to performing it independently.

5. Apprenticeship learning provides opportunities for demonstrating the newly acquired skill. I couldn't wait for my sister to come home from camp and see me riding all by myself. Children can't wait to demonstrate their reading skills to receptive adults, especially teachers and parents.

The Values of Apprentice Learning

Apprentice learning, of course, is not new. What is new is the scientific research on the value of this type of learning, and the growing recognition that American schooling needs to incorporate that value (Antonacci, P. A. and Colasacco, J.M. (1994) or Collins, A., Brown, J.S., and Newman, S.E. eds. (1989). Several features of apprentice learning are thought to underlie its effectiveness and appeal.

Apprentice learning is valued because of its emphasis on authentic and meaningful activity. The apprentice learns by engaging in integrated "real-life" projects or activities, not isolated exercises. Research has shown that people learn best under conditions where they can "make sense" of what they are doing, where learning is not isolated, but embedded in contexts that give it meaning.

Apprentice learning is also of value because of its emphasis on the methodology of instruction. Too much of what passes for teaching is really just the presentation of information—knowledge transfer from the teacher (or the textbook or the video) to the child, followed by testing. Apprentice models assume that meaningful learning requires considerable effort and hands-on practice. That means not only providing many opportunities to read, but reading many different selections in different ways.

Another value of apprentice learning is its emphasis on learning skills rather than facts. In this information age, where enormous amounts of data are available, it is more important to learn the skills required to find information, organize it, and present it, rather than just learn the facts themselves.

Lastly, apprentice learning engages children in a "community of practice." In addition to learning specific skills, apprentices are engaged in the very social process of learning how to learn. From mentors they learn that even experts face problems that they do not know how to solve; that there are "tricks of the trade" and ways to "learn how to learn." They observe that even mentors have mentors; and that the whole community is dependent on many different kinds of mentors. Moreover, the learner joins a community that has values, that has responsibilities that go with competence, and that is continually changing and learning.

Apprentices in Reading

How does apprenticeship fit in a balanced reading program? Apprentice learning can be at the heart of your program. Begin by ensuring that your classroom has enough mentors to demonstrate for every child the "real-life" importance of knowing how to read. As the teacher, you are the foremost mentor, but you may need others. *Variety is key.* Let children see that literacy is important to everyone in their community, from basketball stars to custodians to rocket scientists. Have mentors come to read with children and talk with them about what literacies they need at work. Have them show children what "tricks of the trade" they've learned, even take them to work to see a community of literacy in action.

You can also teach new reading skills by modeling them. Let children hear you "think aloud" as you work to get meaning from a sentence or to sound out a word. The secret of mentoring is to make what is automatic (and thus invisible) for you, observable and obvious for the apprentice.

It is also important to provide scaffolds to help apprentice readers. Shared reading is one example (older students can often be great mentors). Also careful selection of graded material provides scaffolding. New programs and electronic books have supports built into the text that are very helpful for apprentice readers.

Gradually release the scaffolds so that children are more and more independent in their reading. Rereading literature again and again with decreasing support is a valuable part of apprenticing.

Provide lots of opportunities for children to demonstrate the power of their new skills in real-life contexts. Just like at piano recitals and track meets, every child should know that he or she will have the opportunity to demonstrate newly acquired proficiencies.

In a world where the skills of literacy are becoming ever more demanding and where the "age of information" imposes on us the need for broad skills and strategies, we are all finding that we are apprentices again. Children need that opportunity, too.

David Rose is the Founder and Executive Director of the Center for Applied Special Technology (CAST). He is also an educator and clinical psychologist. Rose lectures at Harvard University's Graduate School of Education.

References

Antonacci, P. A. & Colasacco, J.M (1994). A Literacy Context for the 21st Century Child. In N.J. Ellsworth, C.N. Hedley, and A.N. Barata, eds., *Literacy: A Redefinition.* Hillsdale, New Jersey.: Erlbaum.

Collins, A., Brown, J.S., & Newman, S.E. (eds.) (1989). Cognitive Apprenticeship; Teaching the Crafts of Reading, Writing, and Mathematics, in Resnick, L.B. *Knowing, Learning and Instruction* Hillsdale, New Jersey.: Erlbaum Associates 1989.

Spotlight on **PRACTICE**

W e n d y   B r a n d r o w s k i

Classrooms are sometimes artificial places, sealed off from real life. I have found that adopting a mentor model of teaching helps to bring the vitality and excitement of the real world into my classroom. It's there that children must safely and enthusiastically learn to live and to learn.

One School's Experience

Where do you find mentors? Certainly they can be found in the outside community. Last year our school wrote a grant and received funding to engage a local poet who became our Poet in Residence. He was a huge success; virtually the whole school became apprentice poets to this writer.

The year began with a workshop for teachers where we were all engaged in writing poetry, not just learning about it. Under the poet's guidance, and as apprenticed poets ourselves, we experienced what the children would experience.

We then introduced our Poet in Residence to the students at an all-school assembly. Even though the poet would not be working with all of the students individually, we felt it was important for the whole school to learn from him and feel a part of the project. For the fourth- and fifth-graders, the poet came to individual classes to present lessons on writing poetry.

Power of Observation

His style of teaching fit the model we wanted. He didn't lecture about poetry, he showed children how he wrote poetry. Then he engaged children in writing poetry with him. For example, he emphasized the power of observation. To do that, he first demonstrated his own way of looking at things closely, showing his own "tricks of the trade" to help himself see the "essence" of things. Then he had the children practice observation with him.

Writing Process Continues

During the year, class lessons ranged from prewriting to editing. After his lesson, teachers continued the process with their students. In addition, there was another aspect of the mentoring that was a big hit.

Each week the poet would set up a "Poet's Corner" in the hall. Students could drop by, read him their poems, and talk with him about their work. He did not "correct" their poems, but often asked questions that prompted them to think about their work, or shared an observation with them. Students (and teachers) loved the opportunity to meet one-on-one with the mentor.

The year ended with each student contributing one of his or her poems to the school anthology. The anthology was presented to the school in an assembly. There was a celebration and dramatization of the process of writing. Sample poems were read aloud and the anthologies were distributed to everyone. The assembly program and the anthology celebration has become a part of the school culture that continues long after the Poet in Residence's year ended.

Teacher as Mentor

Bringing in an outsider is one way to provide the experience of real-life mentorship, but it is not the only way. Each teacher is, of course, the primary mentor of the classroom. This role can be exaggerated to good effect. Here is an example.

For social studies, my class was studying the southeast region of the United States. This is a region of the country with which I am familiar, having lived there previously.

Rather than tell children about the Southeast, I decided that they would learn more if I engaged them in living a part of the culture. I, as the resident expert, would serve as their mentor.

One day in the middle of a quiet work time, I burst into the classroom in full Mardi Gras regalia. With little elaboration I asked my students to join with me in the celebration of Mardi Gras.

We made floats that represent cultural traditions and artifacts from the region. These products were just like those in the real Mardi Gras, except ours were shoe-box size instead of semitrailer size. Eventually, we got the whole school to join in our celebration of the Southeast—through an evocation, with beads and other details of the Mardi Gras. All my students know how to celebrate, and they learned a lot about the complex culture, traditions, and people of the Southeast.

Look to Older Children, too

There is another source of mentors: the children themselves. Like many schools, we have had great success with older children serving as mentors for younger ones. In poetry, for example, there is a lot that a fourth-grader can do to help a second-grader write a first piece. Fortunately, both students benefit.

Everyone Benefits

Lastly, we have found that there are other mentors everywhere. Through watching our children, our custodian became interested in observing monarch butterflies. Over the summer he carefully observed and recorded many aspects of these creatures' habits and behavior. He then presented to the class his findings—becoming a fabulous mentor as scientist.

Who Are the Apprentices?

All of us. Teachers, staff, and students were all apprentices to the Poet in Residence, for example. It is critical for students to see that their teachers can be apprentices, too. Students observe teachers sitting with the poet in Poet's Corner, and seeking feedback on their own poems. Students see teachers' poems published in an anthology, and understand that teachers value learning.

Similarly, a student learns that he or she can be, at the same time, a mentor to a second-grader in reading, and an apprentice to the custodian in science. They learn that they can begin the week as apprentices to me in the Mardi Gras celebration, but end as mentors on the subject for other students in the school.

The key is not that there is one mentor or teacher, but that there are many. Just as every student should have many chances to be an apprentice, every student should have many chances to be a mentor. Just like in real life.

Wendy Brandrowski teaches in the Cutler School in Hamilton, Massachusetts.

Assessing Your Classroom

(1) Observe your classroom when the children are out of the room.
Are most of the "artifacts" (things on the wall or on desks and tables) items rarely seen elsewhere in real life—for example, worksheets, spelling tests, graded papers, alphabet charts, vocabulary cards?

Or, by contrast, are there plenty of artifacts that are part of real-life settings—reports, completed projects, files of resources, works in progress, calendars and charts, and tools of the trade?

(2) Observe the students in the classroom on a busy day. What kinds of activities occupy most of their time? Are they sitting at desks, watching and listening to you?

Or are they working on isolated skills in workbooks and textbooks?

Or, by contrast, are they working on extended projects that involve real-life skills, from reading to planning to collaborating in writing?

(3) Observe the kind of help that students receive. Do they primarily receive assistance in the form of corrections on papers and other assignments?

Or, by contrast, do they receive help from a mentor (such as you or other students) while they are working?

Does the mentor provide modeling, scaffolding, and feedback, therefore allowing them to succeed?

(4) Reflect on your teaching. Which characterizes your primary form of teaching: lecture? small grouping?

Do students feel free to ask questions?

Or, do you demonstrate the desired skills yourself, provide scaffolds for apprenticing students, guide students toward completion of projects and gradually release the kinds of support provided?

(5) Examine the ways in which you evaluate children's performance.
Do you assess students through tests of specific, isolated skills, or by correcting worksheets?

Or, do you evaluate children's performance through authentic demonstrations, such as those students will be expected to perform when they are older—a report, a speech, a screenplay, a pamphlet, a poster, or a campaign?

Try This

1 **Choose a mentor for yourself.**
A colleague of ours has often chosen high school science teachers as mentors to help him prepare for teaching his own students, and to extend his own learning of science.

Find a teacher who specializes in an area of interest to you. Observe the person at work. Talk with the mentor about his or her activities. Ask about the books the person reads or the mentors he or she has. If possible, ask to borrow some of the person's tools (such as science equipment or artist's brushes).

2 **Choose to be a mentor whenever you can.**
Consider, for example, one of our favorite activities—Living Biography. In this activity, which extends over many weeks, each student reads a biography. Rather than ask students to write a report as a final project, have a big party in which everyone comes as the person they read about. Students can come in costume and stay in character throughout the party, meeting each other and learning about "each other's" life and accomplishments.

A good way for students to get the idea is for you to come dressed as the person you hold as mentor (an outstanding teacher of yours, perhaps, or a musician or artist). To liven up the party, invite parents who also may come as people from the past or present who they most admire.

3 **Invite parents and other members of the community to be mentors.**
Parents and others who have skills often love to share those skills with students; they often provide the best kinds of extended apprenticeships. During a science project, for example, experienced parents can be very helpful as guides for the students during the investigations or afterward, as students extend the activity.

4 **Look for opportunities to make connections.**
During a recent poetry unit students spent a lot of time increasing their powers of observation. The Poet in Residence was particularly helpful in demonstrating to the children how to look closely at simple things to understand them and to get meaning from them.

When you invite a mentor to your classroom, try to make connections between that person's area of interest and other areas of the curriculum. For example, if the mentor is a poet, make connections to science, where close observation is equally vital.

You may even want to invite two mentors to class. Talk to students about what is the same and what is different about what they do. This can be very exciting—even for the mentors.

8

Supporting All Learners

Spotlight On **THEORY**

Hilda Medrano

R ecently I walked into a bilingual education classroom in an elementary school. As I "toured" the room, I noticed children busily engaged in activities. They worked individually and in small groups, moving from one area of the room to another as needed to complete their work. Students interacted with each other as they conferred with classmates about their projects or assignments.

I also observed:

- three children sitting on a carpet, working on independent assignments;

- two other children working at the two computers in the classroom—one girl used a math and reading program, the other practiced for a state mandated test;

- a group of five children sitting at a table using teacher-made Flip Chutes for vocabulary development, and Electro Boards;

- six children gathered around the Listening Center, listening to prerecorded books while following along in the text;

- five students reading with the teacher as she guided them through a selection from a reader;

- two other students under a canopy, using puzzles while discussing careers;

- two students at a computer innovating on a favorite story.

The students seemed independent in their roles and self-assured. As I continued my visit in the room, I noticed students' work displayed in many places: on the walls, hanging from clothespins clipped to a string extending from one corner of the ceiling to another, and on bulletin boards. I also read through their stories (in English and Spanish), which had been made into booklets and placed in the Library Center. I also noticed that there were many labels, such as those for centers or for names of materials, in two languages.

It was clear to me that this was a classroom in which students' needs were well supported. I interviewed the teacher during her conference time to find out her rationale and learn about other practices that meet with success.

The Class Itself

Tell me about your students, I began. She described them as a typical class with a wide range of reading abilities Some had special learning needs. Her classroom included one child diagnosed with Attention Deficit Disorder. Two children with hearing difficulties received services from a speech therapist. A few children were very advanced and needed special challenges to maintain their interest.

Teacher's Techniques

My next question related to her teaching and management. She simply said that she tries to teach in ways that encourage all students to achieve success. It is important to provide the materials and the type of classroom environment that allows all students to learn. She said that it was her job to facilitate learning for all students.

I then asked:

- What do we mean by supporting all learners?

- How can teachers support all learners in their classrooms?

- What research substantiates supporting all learners?

The following is based on that discussion, on talks with other teachers, and on my own research.

Supporting All Learners

ESL Students

For ESL learners some teachers recommend strategies and techniques needed to provide comprehensible input and "context-embedded" (Cummins, 1984) communication.

- ESL learners can be supported by using retellings of text. The teacher can use simple, everyday language to retell segments of text before guiding ESL students through the reading of a story.

- ESL learners can be given prompts to retell stories. Asking children to retell can ensure their comprehension.

- Visuals, such as pictures, also provide excellent ways for supporting ESL learners. Other graphic devices, such as charts, can be used to help students think through story grammar and story lines.

- Helping ESL learners make real-life connections is another way to facilitate their learning.

- Teachers agree that pairing ESL learners with proficient speakers of English is a low-risk and supportive way to include ESL learners in all classroom instruction. In some classrooms this may be "buddy reading" or providing practice with developing skills (such as contractions *he's, she's,* and *I'm*) in real-life context. This involves partners taking turns as they make statements about themselves using contractions ("I'm a boy."/ "You're a girl.").

- Listening to stories read aloud through audiocassettes or on a computer, allowschildren to hear the sound of reading

- Pantomime and role-playing are also low-risk activities for supporting ESL learners.

Special Needs

Mainstream classrooms usually include students who require extra help to comprehend and process information. For these students, teachers can make academic modifications such as:

- dividing tasks between partners;

- using role-playing;

- modeling Think Alouds;

- providing hands-on learning using magnet boards or technology options;

- use computer programs that teach and reinforce reading and writing.

I saw one teacher using a plot diagram to help students summarize a fairy tale. This population of students can also be supported by using games during the teaching-learning process.

How did teachers support learners who require modifications in their teaching because of visual or auditory differences in their learning abilities? Teachers replied that some students require simple, yet effective, ways of accessing information. Teachers recommended:

- helping students chunk information and focusing their attention on chunks or pieces of text at a time;

- using hands-on learning;

- using graphic organizers;

- employing multisensory techniques;

- creating peer partners;

- encouraging think-time and wait-time so children can prepare to express their ideas.

Extra Challenges

At the upper extreme of learning abilities are the students who need extra challenges. I found teachers just as concerned about this student population as with the other diverse learners in the classroom.

Teachers agreed that students who excelled in their classrooms benefited from:

- working in pairs or cooperative groups, especially when reading difficult passages from trade books or library books;

- challenging students to write innovations or parallel story lines for texts they are reading;

- inviting children to write text on the computer and adding illustrations of their own;

- challenging students to create and perform skits for their classmates;

- moving beyond the four walls of the classroom by participating in outside research and projects;

- working with mentors.

How Can Teachers Support All Learners in Their Classrooms?

- Teachers need to draw on an extensive knowledge-base of content, materials, pedagogy, and technology resources so as to provide meaningful learning experiences for all learners.

- Classrooms need to be organized so that they become student-centered communities where all learners feel free to take risks during the teaching and learning process.

- In learner-centered classrooms, instruction is not always directed by the teacher. The teacher sometimes facilitates experiences so that learning is discovered by individual learners or learned collaboratively through strategies such as peer tutoring or cooperative grouping. In classrooms where all learners are *supported,* assessment is for identifying strengths and weaknesses and for guiding instruction, not for marking benchmarks or grades.

- Teachers who support all learners provide active teaching in order to promote active learning.

- Teachers need to see differences among learners as opportunities for cultural exchanges and for providing learning experiences that *support* all learners. This can be done by:
  - promoting cooperative learning;
  - using a variety of resources that promote literacy development, and that teach content, relationships, and central themes of various disciplines.

Balanced reading programs allow teachers and students to listen, speak, read, and write in different contexts and using different texts. As Cambourne (1988) says, learning to become literate ought to be as uncomplicated and barrier-free as possible. He goes on to say that once learned, the skills of literacy should be durable. He explains that when children learn to read and write in classrooms they will continue to use those skills outside the classroom and for the rest of their lives.

What Research Substantiates Supporting All Learners?

On Learning
Cambourne's research on language learning and literacy has identified some principles based on the conditions of learning that seem to make learning to talk successful.

Teachers who understand the principles:

- Arrange their classrooms so that specific conditions of learning are manifested in their classrooms.

- Practice reflection. Teachers reflect on what they plan and teach and, in general, review all interactions they have with all learners. Reflective teachers model and demonstrate to their students learning strategies and strategic reading skills. They also model how to be reflective learners.

On Grouping
Recent research indicates that heterogeneous grouping supports students of low and high ability. Such grouping encourages students to interact and learn from the

background and knowledge each brings to the classroom.

A summary of the research and literature on grouping conducted by O'Donnell and Moore (1980) indicates that homogeneous grouping has not been demonstrated to be an effective method for raising the reading achievement levels of students.

Research indicates that interaction among students of different achievement levels tends to stimulate low achieving students positively (Hayes, 1991). By implementing heterogeneous grouping, and flexible and temporary skills groups, teachers can support learners with different needs and interests.

On Balanced Reading

Research has been conducted on balanced reading programs calling for an integrative approach to reading and language arts instruction, treating the language arts processes (listening, speaking, reading, writing, and viewing) as mutually supportive, not as distinctive subjects.

Balanced reading programs are characterized by different literacy events facilitated by teachers and sometimes by the students themselves. Such literacy events include:

- teacher reading aloud
- shared reading
- guided reading
- sustained independent reading
- journal writing
- language experiences

- reading and writing across the curriculum
- discussions and sharing
- self-selected reading and writing
- choral reading

(Routman, 1991)

Hilda Medrano is Associate Professor, University of Texas—Pan American; Language Arts Consultant; Coordinator: Language, Literacy, and Culture—Accelerated Master's Degree Program for Today's Teachers.

References

Cambourne, B. (1988). *The Whole Story*, New York: Ashton Scholastic.

Cummins, J. (1984). *Bilingualism and Special Education: Issues in Assessment and Pedagogy*, College-Hill.

Hayes, B. L. (1991). *Effective Strategies for Teaching Reading*, Boston: Allyn and Bacon.

Routman, R. (1991). *Invitations: Changing as Teachers and Learners K–12*, New Hampshire: Heinemann.

Spotlight on PRACTICE

Norma Jasso

In this article I describe the ways in which I support the diverse learners in my room—including ESL students, students with special needs, and students who need extra challenge—as they work on various projects and activities based on a popular theme unit.

Starting a Theme Unit

The unit focuses on rain forests. I ask students to tell me what they know about the subject, and I jot down their ideas in the first column of a three column chart entitled K-W-L: K (what you know), W (what you want to know), and L (what you learned).

K	W	L
Some animals there are endangered. (Bk)	What kind of animals live there?	People around the world are trying to save the animals.

I then ask the youngsters to write questions about what they *want* to know about the rain forest ("What kinds of animals live there?") and I record those on the chart (with students' initials next to each comment). Later, after our research, we will talk about what students have learned.

By calling for students' questions, I acquire a better understanding of students' interests: With regard to the rain forest, for example, do they prefer to concentrate on the people who live in different rain forests around the world? On the fish, insects, and birds? On the mammals? On the ecosystem? Based on their responses, and on information about my students' academic strengths, I gather resources (books, videos, audio tapes, charts, pictures) that meet their particular needs.

Focus on Resources

A week or so later, I introduce to the class the resources I've collected. We discuss how these materials can help students with their research and projects. (Students may be writing reports, performing skits, reading or listening to audiotapes, or constructing models.) I then group students and direct them to their respective learning areas.

As youngsters work on their projects, I walk around the room, helping when students request assistance and taking mental and actual notes about students' progress and needs.

In one work section, some youngsters are painting and labeling a mural of the four levels of the rain forest. Ten-year-old Suehadie is painting and labeling the understory (one of the levels) and the animals that thrive there. I assigned Suehadie this project because she benefits from concrete representation of the concepts in the unit. Since Suehadie also enjoys art and working with her hands, her motivation is high.

As Suehadie works, I informally assess her progress. This bright girl accurately labels the four levels of the rain forest. Her understanding of the concepts is good. I jot this down on a computer label and use it as an anecdotal record. At the end of the day I place the information in the girl's portfolio. Later when Suehadie and I conference, I use the documentation to support my observations about her learning.

Meanwhile, a small group of students are constructing animal stick puppets and studying their lines to role-play the characters in *The Great Kapok Tree*. Nine-year-old Moises will play a leopard. With another student's help, he rehearses his lines, using a raspy voice to simulate the roar of the ferocious animal. Why is role-playing a choice activity for Moises? Because his comprehension of the story improves when he has the opportunity to reread the story, listen as his classmates speak their lines, and act out the plot with his entire body. Moises's understanding is reinforced visually, auditorally, and kinesthetically.

In another area of the classroom, a few students complete their terrariums. Others use informational books from the classroom library to write about the importance of a rain forest. Ten-year-old Lydia refers to an informational book to figure out the "best" plants to use in her terrarium. A tactile learner, Lydia works on the terrarium and writes about it in her journal.

And in *This* Corner . . .

Our classroom library center, which is located in one corner of the room, is filled with books in a variety of genres (fantasy, reference, animal stories, biographies, and other nonfiction). For this unit, students sit on bean bags, reading either fiction or nonfiction texts about rain forests. Eleven-year-old Juan Enrique, who arrived from Mexico last year and is just beginning to read English, sometimes has difficulty filtering out distractions. He needs a relaxed, quiet area to comprehend what he reads. He thrives in the library center.

When he finishes a book, Juan Enrique records the title, author, and a short summary of what he learned in his reading log. (His favorite book is *Environment* by David Cook.) Juan places his reading log in his showcase portfolio, which is an expandable folder filled with his best work. By keeping a reading log, Juan helps me and other interested adults stay apprised of his reading level, interests, and the number of books he has read. (Other students maintain reading logs and portfolios, too.)

Weeks later, toward the end of the unit, the class and I reflect on what we learned. We return to the K-W-L chart and record facts and concepts there. We also share projects, admiring one another's work and offering constructive suggestions for improvement.

In the process, I have provided my students—*all* my students—with the materials and the classroom environment that maximizes their learning.

Norma Jasso teaches in the Eisenhower Elementary School in Edinburg, Texas.

References

Cherry, L. (1990). *The Great Kapok Tree: A Tale of the Amazon Rain Forest.*, Orlando, Florida: Harcourt Brace & Co.

Cook, D. (1983). *Environment.* New York: Crown Publishers.

Assessing Your Classroom

	Always	Sometimes	Never
1 As a teacher, do I use these strategies, when appropriate?			
2 Ask students to retell stories read in class.			
3 Provide prompts for retellings.			
4 Provide visuals and graphic devices.			
5 Help students make real-life connections.			
6 Pair ESL learners with proficient English speakers.			
7 Incorporate pantomime and role-playing.			
8 Divide tasks bewteen partners.			
9 Model Think Alouds.			
10 Provide hands-on learning.			
11 Use technology.			
12 Create peer partners.			
13 Use a variety of groupings.			

Try This

1 Assess Your Students and Your Program.

Think about the term "supporting your classroom." Reflect on students in your classroom. Do you have second-language learners? Students with special needs? Students who need extra challenge? For two or three days, keep track of the ways in which you meet the needs of those particular students. What additional strategies from this chapter can you incorporate into your teaching repertoire.

2 Adapt Lessons to Meet Different Needs.

Plan a lesson for teaching a writing skill, such as writing dialogue. As you plan, think of ways you can adapt the basic lesson to support all learners.

For example, to reach ESL students, you might have them act out the dialogue. To reach students with special needs, provide hands-on learning by giving them magnetic boards and having them place quotation marks in the appropriate places. To reach students who need extra challenge, have them create new dialogue with a twist to the story. Evaluate the effectiveness of these strategies.

3 Use of Technology.

Evaluate certain technology programs to determine if they can be used to meet a variety of needs. For example, for students with vision impairment, can the text be enlarged? Can the story be read aloud? For students who need extra challenge, can students innovate on the text? For ESL students, can they record themselves reading aloud, play it back, and compare the read-aloud with the original?

9

English Language Learners

Spotlight on **THEORY**

Alfredo Schifini

Who Are the Students?

Almost every teacher has experienced the challenge of instructing students whose language proficiency is not in English. These children tend to fall into two groups. "ESL students" are those for whom English is a second, usually new, language. In most cases these students are fluent in another language. Limited English Proficient (LEP) is a term commonly used to designate students who are learning in English although it is a second language.

Perhaps more appropriate terms are second-language learners or students acquiring English. These learners vary greatly with regard to language and literacy in their home language, previous exposure to English, and, in some cases, level of prior schooling.

What Are the Goals?

Despite the profound diversity of their backgrounds, these students share common goals and needs.

Literacy

All students must achieve literacy skills in English. In many school settings, literacy development in the student's home language has facilitated achievement of this goal. Increasingly, youngsters have been successful in attaining high levels of literacy in both their native tongue and in English. Students who read and write well in their home language are able to do so at a faster rate in English. At a minimum, however, age appropriate English literacy skills for all youngsters, regardless of the primary language, are the main goal.

Academic Achievement

Access to high-level learning while students are acquiring the English language is also an important goal. Success in academically rigorous instruction ensures that English learners will not fall behind. Also, the more youngsters learn, the more they bring to the task of acquiring English.

Positive Self-esteem

High levels of stress and anxiety impede second-language learning. When students have a positive self-image and are confident, they acquire English easier and excel academically.

What Research Supports English Language Learning?

In recent years there has been a shift in the way we have thought about English language learning. Traditionally, there was a great deal of emphasis in studying specific aspects of the language. Recently, researchers and practitioners have come to agree that language is best taught indirectly through use. Students are encouraged to understand messages in English and to use the language for real purposes. This is in sharp contrast to the study of the language itself. It is thought that a balance of language input from a variety of sources forms a basis for students to begin to produce English. Many sociolinguists have maintained that students can start communicating by using very little amounts of English to negotiate meaning. They have pointed out the need for social interaction and the necessity for students to use the new language even if imperfectly. Lastly, scholars have underscored the need for patience in dealing with English language learning. While the social dimension of English may develop almost immediately, becoming fluent in English takes time.

How Does It All Fit into a Balanced Reading Program?

Students' proficiency in learning English is key to the job at hand. Youngsters may demonstrate a high level of English ability in social settings such as the playground. On the same day, they may experience difficulty in understanding subject matter in class. Understanding English is more difficult when children have little or no background with the new concept. To facilitate rapid growth across the phases of language acquisition, it is necessary to use a variety of instructional approaches and surround the learners with lots of rich language. Literature and other materials with exciting content are wonderful sources.

In many school settings, particularly when large numbers of students speak the same home language, it is feasible to continue native language development and to provide for primary language literacy. In such situations, students receive all the elements of a balanced literacy program in the primary language. As with any quality reading experience, the emphasis is on the construction of meaning with text. Students read many different genres and get practice in writing for a variety of purposes. The four modes of language are integrated, and skills are taught in context. Concomitantly, students learn English. Thus, while their English is evolving, students are forging a high level of literacy.

Often, English learners in a class are few in number or represent several language groups. Even so, it is advisable to continue using the native language as part of the literacy program. When students are very new to English, it is important to allow them to use their native language to express abstract thought and to demonstrate higher-level thinking. English is learned by integrating language and content instruction. Literature and subject matter is embedded in a rich language learning context. You can support this learning with technology, visuals, props, multisensory input, and pair and small group work.

What Kinds of Practices Support English Language Learning?

It is important to remember that students *acquire* a new language and that this acquisition takes place over time. Students' language will develop in a fairly predictable order:

- *Preproduction*, in which children express themselves nonverbally.
- *Early Production*, in which children give one- or two-word responses.
- *Speech Emergence*, in which students give short answers.
- *Intermediate Fluency*, in which students express more abstract concepts.

As you work with English learners in these different stages, keep the following "do's and don'ts" in mind:

DO:

- let the language develop naturally by modeling and demonstrating new vocabulary and constructions.
- create lots of opportunities for children to use the language by allowing them to experiment.

- keep in mind that motivation and anxiety greatly affect language learning.

- build on prior experience and background.

- encourage home language use.

- use sensitive strategies in correcting errors.

- celebrate good guesses and treat grammatical/phonological errors as normal signs of growth.

- encourage use of the new language, even if imperfect.

- recognize that learners understand more language than they can produce.

- combine verbal and nonverbal input (describe, demonstrate, model, and talk through activities).

- surround students with lots of language and expect lessons to be more teacher-centered at the beginning stages.

- learn to stretch students' proficiency by providing comprehensible input at slightly above their current level.

DON'T:

- emphasize grammar in the beginning stages.

- drill and practice new forms of the language in isolation.

- pressure students to perform individually.

- force students to speak prematurely.

- expect full-blown grammatically correct utterances in the beginning.

With time, practice, and an abundance of literacy nourishment, your English language learners will move from stage to stage on the road to fluency.

Alfredo Schifini is Professor, Curriculum and Instruction, California State University, Los Angeles.

Spotlight on **PRACTICE**

Erminda Garcia

The 3R's of Teaching English Language Learners

At one time, as an elementary school student, I understood the 3R's to be reading, writing and 'rithmetic. Today the students in my classroom understand that the 3R's mean respect, response, and resource. These are the behaviors we practice throughout the school day.

My entire teaching experience has been in classrooms where the majority of the students speak a language other than English. During the first day of school, they brainstorm how they can be a resource to one another. We discuss how each child brings a language filled with experience and family stories to the class. We also discuss the cooperative structures and literacy strategies we will be using in class so that we can be more responsive to each other. For example, sitting in groups of four supports listening and speaking as we become language models for each other. We talk about the need to respect the classroom environment as well as the space and property of others. I stress that an important part of the environment is waiting, listening, and trying to understand a different language. I emphasize that when any member of the classroom community speaks, reads, or writes, it is not just a set of sounds, syllables, or parts, but words with purpose and meaning.

Respect

I believe respect comes through giving children a choice of what they would like to learn about. I offer them a choice of reading and writing materials, and allow them to work in the language or languages that they choose. My students see their choices in materials on the walls, in our classroom books, and through the learning themes that we use. Each student is respectful of other students whether or not they speak, read, or write the same language.

During the first few weeks, students bring in the kinds of things that they are able to read: books, logos, bills, newspapers, and letters. As students discuss how difficult a language might sound or look, they are often surprised at the similarities among languages. I respect their approximations in reading and writing and use these to help me plan my next instructional move.

Finally, I am respectful to each child by keeping my expectations high for each one.

Response

I believe that learning is a social activity and have structured the learning opportunities in my classroom around this belief. The cooperative structures and many of the literacy strategies that we use allow us to respond to each other in many ways. When children sit to hear a story that is being read to them, they pair up to discuss what meaning they are constructing. During these literature conversations, I stop and ask questions that call for personal interpretation as well as predictions. These authentic responses initiate conversations about story lines and predictions, and often create safe places to try English as children react to each others' comments. Similar responses occur in shared-reading and shared-writing groups.

In these situations, the response for clarification is not, "you say it like this," or "the correct word to use is," but "I don't understand what you mean, read it again." All of the students can participate in context while acquiring English in a responsive manner. The use of cooperative structures allow language buddies to create authentic uses of English. I continually foster reflection on how children respond to each other ("Did you sound out the word? Did you talk about how the words sound or look a lot alike?").

Resources

In a classroom, students and teachers bring many kinds of resources to one another. Each brings the resources of family, the experiences they have provided, and the traditions in which they participate. I see my role as helping children seek out these resources through books, through home surveys, through their writings, and most importantly, by understanding the value of the resource they will have in future years. For example, in one activity we created a storyboard where parents were asked to think of language events or words for the eight years of their child's life. The magnificent memories of all the parents enabled my students to share for hours how they had learned to talk, read, and write. They discussed who taught them, when they stopped "baby talk," and who in their homes could speak, read, or write in more than one language. This in turn prompted an inquiry into how the brain stores more than one language.

Of particular interest to me is the resource of language. After so many years of working with students who are acquiring English, I build their learning opportunities and my teaching on their primary language and continually use it as a resource. When learning reflects the resources in the classroom, it is no surprise that the richness is reflected, too.

A Specific Learning Context

Every day, my class engages in interactive partner journals. At the beginning of each month, the students list at least three children to whom they would like to write. I then make final selections based on partners who can become language, knowledge, or interest resources for each other. During the day, partners write to each other, always responding to the meaning of their messages and often to some of the written mechanics. They choose their own topics and text. As a member of the community, I am one of the partners.

This context provides clear examples for English language learners of how their responses become resources for others. As my English language learners begin to approximate English in print, writing words or one or two sentences with sound symbol connections, their partners respond in English. You can almost hear the English learners thinking, If she or he thinks I can read in English, then I must be able to write in English. They have become users of English in a context where the 3R's have created optimal learning for them.

Erminda Garcia teaches at the Alianza School in Watsonville, California.

Assessing Your Classroom

In assessing your own program, consider the following:

English Language Development	Yes	Some	No
1 Are students getting specific lessons in a program for second-language learners so that they may acquire social and academic English?			
2 Are all the materials being used for that purpose of high quality?			
3 Are the lessons relevant and purposeful?			
4 Do the lessons proceed from whole to part?			
5 Is the input embedded with contextual support (visuals, props, audiovisual help, charts)?			
6 Do students use the English they are acquiring to carry out activities with English-speaking peers (especially during art, music, physical education, and other activities)?			
Subject Matter In English			
1 When instruction is in English, are students understanding and participating?			
2 Are the students demonstrating that they grasp the concepts in a variety of ways (drawing, making a product, using or applying the concept other than solely writing about it)?			
Primary Language			
1 Do students who are new to English receive language arts and subject matter in the home language?			
2 Does the staff hold high expectations for the LEP students?			
3 Do the LEP students and mainstream students interact?			

Try This

① Routines as Literacy Lessons

Use routines as literacy lessons for students acquiring English. For example, taking attendance, weather reports, and calendar activities can be modeled and assigned so that the leader or student of the day exercises leadership and learns by repeating a routine. This type of literacy lesson promotes language development and literacy in a supportive environment.

Think about the routines you currently use in your classroom. Select one and determine how you can use it as a literacy lesson. Try it out and then evaluate its effectiveness. Try another!

② Students as Mentors

Children can learn a great deal from one another—especially those learning a new language. Start a mentor program in your classroom. Survey the children in your class to find their area of expertise. Some are great at editing while others read aloud well. Still others are very good at giving directions, helping with class chores, or solving problems. Include all the children on your expert list. Post the list in your classroom and encourage children to use one another's expertise. After several weeks, reevaluate your mentor program. How is it working? What are the benefits? What changes do you need to make? Encourage feedback from the children during your reevaluation.

10

Using Technology in Your Classroom

Spotlight on **THEORY**

David Rose

From Plato to the Present

Centuries ago, Plato fretted about a new technology called writing. He saw the written word as a threat to the highly developed art of oratory. If writing were widely adopted, thought Plato, students would focus on it, and the skills of oratory would suffer. In 1703, teachers worried about another new technology—the writing slate. If students depended on a slate, the argument went, they would lose the skill of preparing bark for writing and thus be unable to write when they broke a slate. In 1928, the *Rural American Teacher* reported another worry: students were depending too much on store-bought ink. They no longer knew how to make their own.

Today we are at a juncture that Plato would have recognized. Teachers are still concerned about the role of technology in the classroom, particularly about its impact on the development of literacy.

As Plato predicted, technology does create changes. The art of oratory did decline as the technology of writing flourished. Education became dominated by reading and writing. In the centuries that followed, students had to learn both the technical and cognitive skills to communicate effectively through this new concept of literacy.

What Plato and others failed to recognize was the "upside"—the great power of the new literacy. Although modern "Platos" may worry that, in the digital world of television, computers, and video games, literacy will be eroded, in fact, the opposite is already proving true—literacy has assumed a greater role than ever before.

Lessons to Learn

There are three things to learn from Plato's era.

1. *It is a mistake to ignore the power in new technologies.* Writing in Plato's era was not just a distraction from "real" communication (oratory), it was an expansion of what "real" communication could be. By clinging to the power of the old technologies, we often fail to see the possibilities and power in the new, to see that the concept of literacy itself is changing.

2. *It is a mistake to ignore the power in existing technologies.* The replacement of oral culture with written culture need not have happened. In Plato's time, recognition that both spoken and written communication are vital would have resulted in an expanded concept of literacy. By viewing new technologies as replacements for old, we shortchange ourselves and our culture.

3. *Don't fail to consider that young people, particularly children, are not afraid of new technology.* Indeed, they are often more successful with it than adults. (To whom do you turn for help in programming the VCR?) Nor do young people harbor preconceived fears about the impact of new technology whether it be writing on a slate or using store-bought ink. By tapping their interest and channeling the use of new technology, teachers can enlist a powerful tool in the literacy process. Just as Plato's students learned writing, modern children quickly pick up the ever-changing technology of today.

Technology in Balanced Reading

What is the role of technology in a balanced reading program? The lesson to learn from Plato's era is that such a question is too narrow. We need to look instead at the role of technology in a balanced *literacy* program. Ever since Gutenberg made movable type, the role of technology has been central to literacy and thus to all of our teaching. The question we now face is about the *choice* of technologies—what technology will be central to our culture and to our teaching?

A balanced literacy program requires that children learn to use both old and new technologies to communicate. They must learn to speak and to listen without any technology at all. They must learn to read and write with old technologies such as paper and pencil. They must also learn to read and write and speak and listen with new technologies such as the Internet.

More importantly, children need to learn when to use each kind of technology—when to speak, when to use paper, when to use sound recording, when to use video, or when to use images combined with text.

Classroom Practices

What classroom practices will support the development of a truly balanced literacy?

1. *Create a classroom environment that reflects the real world.* Put in this environment the most prominent communication technologies that are available and support them. Such an environment should include books, of course, and other technologies for a balanced literacy. Computers, video player, audio, and connections to the network should all be on hand.

2. *Provide modeling and mentoring for a balanced literacy by utilizing both old and new technologies in your teaching, and in your own work.* Just as children should see (and hear) you read from books, they should see you read (and hear) from such diverse sources as electronic encyclopedias, an Egyptian Web Page, or a video on Martin Luther King. They should see you work to write a note, to send a message over the network, compose a poster on paper or on the computer screen, or create a collage of images and words. If you feel uncomfortable with a new technology, let one of the children take the lead. Children love to show off their knowledge, and they benefit from seeing that others, especially their mentors, are learners.

3. *Find opportunities to demonstrate the similarities and differences between the various technologies.* As Douglas Hartmann would recommend, "read across texts," showing and comparing, for example, both the book and video versions of *The Red Balloon.* You could show two stories by the same author, one in software, the other in print. Encourage children to use both an electronic encyclopedia and a printed encyclopedia and help them see the strengths and weaknesses of each. Let them present their projects in various media over the year—orally, in text, on the computer screen, on video.

4. *Use the power of new technologies to help teach old literacies.* For example, use the power of multimedia electronic books to help children learn to read regular books. Record speeches by children so that they can critique them (and edit them if you have the appropriate equipment). Let children browse in areas of interest on the Internet (or more protected network), and then select their own material for reading. Use gaming software that is fun but requires on-screen reading to succeed.

In the Future

What are the results of using technology with a balanced literacy program? Long-term results are not yet available, but there are many research and theoretical articles to support such an effort. These emphasize the changing nature of our literacies and classrooms. The new tools, and the practices outlined here, will help ensure that you create a balanced literacy program—one that prepares children not only for using the technologies of the past, but the technologies of their future.

David Rose is the Founder and Executive Director of the Center for Applied Special Technology (CAST). He is also an educator and clinical psychologist. Rose lectures at Harvard University's Graduate School of Education.

References

For a recent article about the promise of multimedia in the classroom, see "New Ways to Learn" by Andy Reinhardt (*Byte Magazine*, March 1995).

For articles on teaching literacy with the new technology, see "Turned on to Language Arts: Computer Literacy in the Primary Grades" by Larry Guthrie and Susan Richardson (in *Educational Leadership*, October 1995) or "The New Literacy: Beyond the Three R's" by M. Hill (*Electronic Learning*, September 1992).

For articles that examine how the new technologies are changing our schools, see "The Role of Computer Technology in Restructuring Schools" by A. Collins (*Phi Delta Kappan*, September 1991) or any of a large number of articles in a special issue of *Educational Leadership* called "How Technology is Transforming Teaching" (October 1995).

Spotlight on **PRACTICE**

Mark Williams

I was a librarian before I was a teacher. Some people think of librarians as "book people," but it was as a librarian that I first learned about the rapidly changing technologies of information and literacy. In a modern library it is no longer possible to think of books or printed materials as the exclusive sources of information, or of card catalogs as the fundamental mechanism for searching for information—even for books. Instead, any library, like any business, uses multiple technologies for getting information, for keeping knowledge, and for communicating.

My Early Goals

When I became a teacher, I was struck by how different classrooms were from the real world of libraries and businesses. While most teachers had a computer in the room, and there was a computer laboratory in the building, the new technologies were not central to what was going on in classroom. I felt I wanted to make my classroom a place where children learned about all of the kinds of technologies that could help them to learn, think, and communicate in a balanced literacy program.

I started by physically changing my classroom to reflect the importance of technology. I moved the two Macintosh computers from the back of the room to the center of the room. (I now have three Macs). There I created a central work area from which I could teach, and children could learn. The children's desks, and other work areas, surround this central location.

Children sometimes use the computers on their own, and sometimes I use one of them by myself. We do the most important things together. The key tool for working together is the projection plate—a device that is placed on the overhead projector in my room and which allows me to show everyone in the class what is on my computer screen. I use this system for a great deal of my teaching. Let me give an example.

Computers and Writing

As part of my writing program I use technology to help me model the process of writing for the students, to provide scaffolds for the collaborative process of writing, and to provide a common focus of attention and effort.

A Computer "Outline"

To be specific, I might begin the process of writing with a group brainstorm session. I use a program that allows me to accept ideas from students, display them visually on the screen, move around words and sentences easily, and turn the work into the basis for an organized essay or story.

I like this program because it is a visual—as opposed to a primarily verbal—tool like the traditional outline. I find it effective because its visual nature supports many kinds of learners. Children can easily see the way things can be grouped to make a larger unit, the way these larger units can be connected or related, and the way these various relationships can be regrouped and reconnected. With the projection plate we can do this exercise together and we see the results together as well.

I usually lead the lesson from the keyboard, but a student can lead as well. Other children contribute from their desks. Everyone can follow our collaborative process on the projection screen, but I also distribute paper so that children can write down what is happening. This group process of writing, aided by the computer and projection plate, allows me to draw every child into the shared writing, and allows me to teach actively and creatively.

Using Multiple Technologies

During other parts of the writing process, children use multiple technologies. At any one time, some children are drafting their work on paper, others entering text on the word processor. Still others are looking for information on a CD, while other youngsters are preparing illustrations. Together we produce a class newspaper.

Reading can also be done with multiple technologies. Certainly, we read lots of books, but children use their computers to read as well, using things like an electronic encyclopedia.

Most important to me is the use of the new technology to help students who are having trouble with reading. I use a program which is highly structured and supportive in phonics—much more than a workbook could ever be because it can "speak" out loud and draw attention to features such as letter to sound correspondence (example: long o or -ate ending).

One of the strengths of using multiple technologies is the capacity to reach more children. I find that some youngsters are not gripped by textbooks. These students need a more engaging route into literacy, and they respond more strongly to less traditional styles of learning. The interactive nature of multiple technologies—with their strong sounds and graphics—interest many of these children, helping them learn to read, and learn to learn.

Goals for the Future

While I am continuing to build a balanced program of literacies, I am still looking for other tools that can help me reach that goal. I have just received a scanner (the first in our school) and our class newspaper is beginning to show the results.

What I really want to do now is connect to the Internet, and to other classrooms, so that my students can communicate with the larger world—both to get information, and to give it.

I feel strongly that this kind of balanced literacy is critical to my students' education. I want to prepare them for the future so they're not trapped in the past.

Mark Williams teaches in the Winthrop School in South Hamilton, Massachusetts.

Assessing Your Classroom

		Yes	Some	No
1	Does the physical layout of your classroom and the technologies available reflect a balanced literacy program? Is there a balance between print technology and other technologies that is reflective of the real world?			
2	When you seek content for a classroom project or activity (for example, for a unit on Antarctica), do you compile materials from a balanced set of media—books, articles, videos, interactive software, Internet home pages?			
3	When you provide extra practice for students having difficulty or extension activities for students who are advanced, do you seek experiences across a balanced set of media that includes print and electronic sources?			
4	When student expression is evaluated, do you ensure that students are judged in terms of their capacities in different media (for example, in writing, in speaking, in illustration, in film, in electronic media, and so forth)?			
5	When you teach students how to find information, do you demonstrate a balanced set of search procedures (for example, using a card catalog, using indexes in print or electronics, using Internet browsers, using CD-ROM information sources)?			
6	Do you demonstrate to your class a balanced set of literacies?			
7	Do you provide students with many ways of accessing information (books, technology, interviews, and so forth)?			
8	Do you actively build on all students' strengths by providing many ways of learning (through books, through audiocassettes, CD-ROMs, and so forth)?			

Try This

(1) Try a thought experiment. Ask yourself: What kinds of technology should my students know how to use in order to be literate in their culture? Then ask yourself: How does my classroom, as it stands now, reflect what they will need? Finally, ask: How should I change my classroom in order to prepare children for *their* future, not for *my* past?

(2) Be exploratory and experimental with new technology. Choose a program that looks promising. Gather the students around you (or use a projection plate) and "dive right in." Try things out just to see what will happen. Walk through the program together with students, and don't be afraid to invite students to help you. Let the students see that even a teacher learns new things, and even teachers ask for help. Children need to see that it's fine with you to be a novice at a new skill. Model how you learn.

(3) Use drill and practice software. We use programs to build basic skills. While this kind of learning should not dominate the classroom, it can be valuable for many students. Kids love it, and you can feel comfortable giving students the time to strengthen their skills. Look in magazines like *Technology and Learning* for reviews.

(4) Use "real" word processors. There is a tendency among teachers to use child-centered programs for writing. I have.

This year, however, I am shifting to a word processor geared for adults. My students have not had any trouble with it, and have taught me some new tricks along the way. Remember, few pieces of software for adults are as intricate as the most basic video game.

(5) When working on a big project, assign leadership and supportive roles, then teach a small group of students a new technology skill. Those few students will teach their classmates. When preparing our class newspaper, I assign leadership roles for the whole project, including the Editor-in-Chief, and then assign teams of students to each leader. I rotate teams and leaders from one issue to the next. Within each team there is usually at least one student who knows how to use a particular technology. Regardless, you can work with one team around a specific technology, then the skill will be taught to classmates in no time at all.

11

Connecting Families and School

Spotlight on **THEORY**

Arlene Mitchell

Build a Home-School Partnership

Through our studies in learning processes and home literacy, we have become increasingly aware that children's preparation for learning and their attitudes about school are influenced by the home environment. Also children's experiences in the classroom and school building affect their home life. It is clear, therefore, that to optimize learning, home and school activities should supplement each other in realistic and positive ways.

To maintain constructive home-school connections both teachers and parents have important responsibilities. Teachers, for example, need to offer suggestions to parents for approaches or activities that may extend the learning process at home. This can be accomplished through letters—in different languages—about reading units, skills, and strategies children are learning. Educational materials families may not be familiar with, such as portfolios and literacy logs, should be described and their functions explained.

Teachers should work toward helping parents feel trust in the school and its staff. Many parents, regardless of socioeconomic status, may feel like outsiders in the process if they perceive that suggested activities are dictates from the teachers. Teachers, therefore, can offer not just one but a variety of suggestions for activities that parents can do with children before and after school and on weekends. The best activities will be those that engage families from a week to several months.

Parents have important roles as well. Parents need to ask their children questions about what they are learning, and be informed by the teacher of expectations in the classroom (homework due dates, special events that require preparation). Then they can help their children succeed with assignments. Parents need to find ways to learn of their children's joys and frustrations so they can recognize, and appropriately reward, foster, sympathize, and supplement. In addition, parents can inform teachers of changing family constructs, such as a new baby or the illness or death of a relative, friend, or pet. These changes may affect the child's behavior. Happy events, such as receiving a special gift, could be shared with the class.

Integrate Learning Concepts into Planned Home Activities

How can teachers cultivate good communication between school and home? They need to build time, opportunity, and flexibility into their program to reach parents. They can create a home-school repertoire of activities that will be energizing for students and parents. (Having a buddy teacher with whom the teacher shares successful approaches also helps.)

Teachers should take time during the school day to explain the home project and organize homework assignments so that children have ample time to participate in the project after class. Home connections should be validated on an ongoing basis. For example, a story read in class may include a request that students retell the story to family members at home. Children would be encouraged to talk the next day about that experience ("My mom said I told the folktale with a good strong voice."). An appropriate connection has been made.

One question parent groups often ask us is, "How can I help my child with homework?" I define homework as school assignments or lesson practice, to be done at home. These are important assignments that prepare children for classroom review and assessment. I suggest that parents:

- read over and talk with their children about homework assignments;

- read aloud to their children;

- listen to their children read aloud;

- encourage opportunities for problem solving and to actively develop children's decision-making skills.

I also encourage parents to provide daily time for "family connections." This is a time that integrates home activities with concepts children are learning in school. Some ideas would include:

- sharing information about the day;

- writing notes to each other as a means of communication;

- reading the newspaper aloud—this reinforces reading skills;

- discussing topics of interest over dinner or while doing dishes.

Sharing Fun Activities

How can children share games and fun activities with siblings and extended family members? Parents can try these suggestions.

- Ask their children to read maps while taking a bus or train ride to a department store.

- Ask their youngsters to mentally or mechanically estimate the cost of groceries to be bought in the grocery store.

Teachers can suggest that students:

- Interview family members or gather information about older or distant relatives for a family history, or they can discuss family goals and dreams.

In short, it is important that, as much as possible, activities that relate to school are woven into normal family activities. Activities that are integral to routines (such as grocery shopping) and recreational (such as traveling on vacation) are more meaningful and more productive to learning than mere add-ons (such as asking a mother how many siblings she has).

Everyone Wins

Children in grades 3–6 begin to develop routines about school and attitudes about learning that influence them throughout their lives. Positive experiences during that time, along with successful outcomes, will encourage children to stay in school. When both home and school environments are working collaboratively, children see connections between what they do in school and how they spend the rest of their time. This knowledge brings meaning to learning.

Arlene Harris Mitchell is Associate Professor of Literacy and English Education; head of the division of Teacher Education at the University of Cincinnati.

Spotlight on **PRACTICE**

G l a d y s   G r a h a m

I teach students in grades 4-6 in an inner-city school in Cincinnati, Ohio. As in many communities, the families' makeup varies greatly. Some students come from single-parent families; others, two-family households; still other students are raised by extended family members such as grandparents or aunts.

Recently, in an attempt to create a more powerful bond between families and school activities, I asked myself several crucial questions about my class, including:

- What are the needs of my students' families?

- How do students interact with their families?

- What interests do students share?

I planned to get the answers to these questions, then use the information to guide me in creating a successful balanced reading development program in my classroom.

An Enlightening Discussion

Through discussion, I learned that for many families, time plays in important role in how parents or caregivers interact with children. For example, some parents work in the evenings, returning home from work at 7 P.M. or as late as 11 P.M., well after children are asleep. Clearly, when suggesting activities in which families can engage, I would have to offer activities that lend themselves to flexible timetables.

A second issue that arose concerned large families. Since there are often many children in the family, I would have to consider that older siblings, not just adults, may be called on to help younger ones with homework and other projects.

At a later time, I held a group family meeting in which I asked families and students for suggestions about how we could connect our literacy learning to their homes. The discussion was successful on many levels. Not only did we collaborate and come up with some excellent ideas, but the interaction created a sense of community and trust. I believe it also set up a positive interaction style for problem solving.

The discussion led to plans for months of family-based reading and writing activities which I will now describe.

Health News Magazine

Our health news magazine included articles on topics of importance to families, such as diabetes, smoking, nutrition, and adequate sleep.

We started by reading newspapers from the community, focusing on content, layout, writing styles, headlines and bylines, and possible sources of information (government bureau of statistics, for example).

Students then generated their own topics for each of several issues, ranging from sports health to female health issues. To generate other topics, students were asked to interview family members to discover health issues that concerned them, such as alcoholism or Alzheimer's disease. (To help students with their interviews, we brainstormed appropriate questions in class on the afternoon before the assignment.)

To produce the first issue, we broke into small groups to do research. This also produced many in-class lessons, ranging from how to use a table of contents, an index, a dictionary, and an encyclopedia. We also studied different kinds of information sources, such as medical books, journal and magazine articles—even telephone books!

Once the research was over, the children then conducted interviews. (Research, interviewing, and writing took about three weeks.) Interviews were conducted as home assignments. Typical questions included: "Mrs. Jones, how often do you provide green vegetables for your family? Where do you do your shopping?" For editing of the articles, we used peer editing in which classmates used a teacher-generated checklist to edit one another's work.

For our second issue we included a Letter to the Editor column in which parents and other family members responded to the articles in the previous issue. We also encouraged parents to write their own articles or to donate time, when possible, to photocopy or print the class magazine.

One thing I learned from this experience is the importance of patience and reflection, and the acceptance of complications as part of the process. Not everything went as planned. We sometimes had to redo assignments and spend more time than expected teaching mini-lessons and readdressing writing skills.

Overall, though, children were often so enthusiastic about working on the magazine that they often gave up part of their lunchtime or came to school early or stayed late to work as a group to finish the articles, layout, or art. Clearly, this project was a great success.

Family Journal Writing and Responding

The purpose of family journal writing is to create a written and spoken dialogue between children and parents, and to use that as a springboard for instruction in the classroom.

I assign family journal writing about two or three times a month. In general, I pose a question and ask children to interview family members for responses. Children write family members' responses in the journal, return to school, and share selected answers.

Recently, my class and I read Virginia Hamilton's *The House of Dies Drear*, a novel that focuses on the history of slavery in the United States, on family history, and on migration. The book generated much talk about families' history of migration from the South, as well as other issues. Children discussed the book with their families, then posed questions. Children wrote family members' responses in the journal, then returned to class to share some points. In the future I hope to expand the family journal writing project by having families respond in writing to the journal or notes of other families.

I learned many things from this activity. Most important, I found that both teacher and students must reflect on the process and product frequently and consistently. This assures that our mutual objectives are being met.

On a positive note, the biggest achievement resulting from this activity is that my most reluctant students are writing more now. They are engaged in the homework assignments and are more productive, which helps in my assessment of their progress. Dialoging between family members and between students helps students realize that they *do know* something on a given subject. In addition, my students are more willing to discuss a topic verbally, and to create a written text of information.

Best of all, family journal writing proved to us that teachers, writers, family members, and community members can be a resource to us all.

Gladys Graham teaches in the Losantville School in Cincinnati, Ohio.

References

Hamilton, V. (1984). *The House of Dies Drear.* New York: Simon & Schuster.

Assessing Your Classroom

	Yes	Some	No
1 Do I include some assignments in which children read to family members or talk to family members about stories?			
2 Have I provided opportunities for children to write about home experiences through free writing, summarizing, informational writing, descriptive writing, and storytelling?			
3 Have I shared ideas with parents that will help children develop thinking and problem-solving skills?			
4 Have I tied home activities to in-school lessons on a weekly basis?			
5 Have I gathered information from parents to help me understand students' learning styles?			
6 Have I kept parents informed of the type of assessments I use (formative and summative; formal and informal; print and nonprint) as well as the content we are studying?			
7 Have I shared ideas with parents that include children's home practice and other activities to assure continuous learning?			
8 Have I found a variety of ways to communicate with the parents of my students? (Examples: Do I make telephone calls, write individual notes, or publish a newsletter?)			
9 Do I involve students in this process?			
10 Have I encouraged parents to inform me of their children's problems or special needs?			

Try This

1 Encourage Parental Involvement.

In preparation for your next theme unit, write an informal letter to families, outlining what the children will be studying and asking for their help. Could parents, grandparents, or older siblings give a talk or presentation that relates to the unit? Could they supply resources (such as videos, magazines) that relate to the theme? Do their hobbies or interests or jobs relate to the theme? If so, is there some aspect that relates to the unit that the family member can share with the class?

2 Getting Ready for Conferences.

For your next family–teacher conference, have students prepare a portfolio of their work, and invite students to participate in the conference. Students should be prepared to talk during the conference about what they learned in the last several months, areas in which they do well, and their goals for the next quarter.

3 Meet With Colleagues.

Meet with staff members and brainstorm the ways you now involve parents in your literacy program. Evaluate the list to see what is working well. Come up with one new way to encourage families to participate (such as Family Literacy Night, Grandparents Night, Read-a-Thon, or contributing to a newsletter). Plan another meeting several months later to evaluate what worked. Share your ideas with another school in the district.